LIVING SUPERNATURAL IN THE NATURAL WORLD
Never Underestimate Your Ability

Diane Wargalla

Testimonial

"One might be tempted to think, when reading the real-life accounts in this book, that Diane must somehow be "different" or "lucky" to have something that only a few ever get. Nope. Diane is like any of us.

Although, I confess, she does have at least 1 superpower that I can attest to. Her laugh is so full of joy and vibrant heart energy, that even the so-called dead take notice! No doubt this is part of the reason she has such magical experiences.

This glimpse into her world, is a portal through which we can enter, realize our own abilities, and apply them practically in our situations same as she does, by being led from our courageous heart; knowing that miracles are not the exception. Indeed, they are the norm and each of us is blessed with superpowers."

- **Christopher Tims,** Order Of the Blue Star, Florida, U.S.A

Living Supernatural in the Natural World: Never Underestimate Your Ability

www.dianewargalla.com
Copyright © 2018 Diane Wargalla

ISBN: 978-1-77277-215-9

All rights reserved. No portion of this book may be reproduced mechanically, electronically, or by any other means, including photocopying, without permission of the publisher or author except in the case of brief quotations embodied in critical articles and reviews. It is illegal to copy this book, post it to a website, or distribute it by any other means without permission from the publisher or author.

Limits of Liability and Disclaimer of Warranty
The author and publisher shall not be liable for your misuse of the enclosed material. This book is strictly for informational and educational purposes only.

Warning – Disclaimer
The purpose of this book is to educate and entertain. The author and/or publisher do not guarantee that anyone following these techniques, suggestions, tips, ideas, or strategies will become successful. The author and/or publisher shall have neither liability nor responsibility to anyone with respect to any loss or damage caused, or alleged to be caused, directly or indirectly by the information contained in this book.

Publisher
10-10-10 Publishing
Markham, ON
Canada

Printed in Canada and the United States of America

Table of Contents

Dedication	v
Acknowledgements	vii
Foreword	ix
Chapter 1 – The Power of Empty	1
Chapter 2 – Change the Weather, Save Your Life	7
Chapter 3 – Meditation: The Original Social Media	25
Chapter 4 – Who Says It's Impossible?	49
Chapter 5 – Continuum: When Does Life Begin or End?	63
Chapter 6 – Now You See Me, Now You Don't	81
Chapter 7 – Resetting Your GPS: Empowering Your Ability to Choose	91
Chapter 8 – Clyde's Story – What a High Vibrational Life Looks Like	103
Chapter 9 – They Said Nothing Happened – They Lied	131
Chapter 10 – Why Increase Your Body Frequency and How?	145
Conclusion	159
Testimonials	167
About the Author	177

Dedication

*This book is dedicated to my two amazing sons,
who have taught me so much about courage,
and hold the space of love and support
for me to be my authentic self.*

Acknowledgements

While my name gets to be on the cover, there are many others who have played an integral role in getting this book to print. A simple 'thank you' would not seem to be enough reward for the help provided, so perhaps seeing your names in print will be.

To Raymond Aaron and his amazing team, for providing the technical support and expertise.

Daniel Cout, for providing a safe haven to share a fresh perspective of the world.

Jack Di Nardo, for his many levels of support and relentless editing, which made it possible to get this book done.

Tracy Knepple, for helping me put word to paper, for your words of encouragement, keeping me organized and on task.

Bob McConkey, for your healthy skepticism, caring supportive nature, and insightful suggestions for the book cover.

Mandy McLaughlin, for being my sounding board. Your words of encouragement helped keep me grounded.

To the Grand R.E.B.A., the most self-aware individuals I have ever met. I thank you for providing the inspiration and conviction to write this book.

My final thoughts belong to my clients and to all of you who attend my workshops: Thank you for the privilege of allowing me to share the empowerment that lives within you.

Foreword

What if you had the ability to see beyond your limited five senses and create from a larger Spirit World where more is possible?

In *Living Supernatural in the Natural World: Never Underestimate Your Ability*, Diane Wargalla reveals that much more is possible than we can even imagine if we only know how to open to it.

In her compelling personal account, Diane transports you out of the everyday world and into the multi-dimensional Spirit World where telepathy and communication with spirits are accessible. She shares her own colorful journey of connecting to the Spirit World and vividly brings her experiences to life. Through this book, you'll have the opportunity to look at the world with a new and powerful perspective in which you can feel more supported in both seen and unseen ways.

Along with her personal experiences, Diane offers practical exercises to help you develop your own ability to communicate with the spirit world. You will deepen your understanding of your connection with others and with the natural world around you.

As we each tap into our ability to communicate with the world beyond what our eyes can see, we expand our insight and express our potential to create a life of greater happiness and a world of greater peace. That is the gift that *Living Supernatural in the Natural World* offers. Enjoy.

Marci Shimoff
#1 *NY Times* Bestselling Author,
Happy for No Reason and *Chicken Soup for the Woman's Soul*

Chapter 1

The Power of Empty

It was a sunny Saturday morning when the Universe gave me a giant wake-up call! The wake-up call came in the form of a minivan, travelling seventy miles per hour, and ramming into the back of my stopped car at a red light. Police reports noted there were no skid marks or other attempts to avoid the collision in what was a clear, crisp, and sunny winter morning. The roads were dry, and driving conditions were perfect.

I worked and lived in Mississauga, Ontario, at the time of the collision, and was on my way to the office with a box of donuts for my team who were covering the phones for a Saturday morning shift. I wanted to support them and show my appreciation for their hard work by showing up with some coffee and donuts! I never made it!

My car responded to the impact exactly as the car designers had intended, by folding together like an accordion, with me staying strapped in the driver's seat. One moment I was changing the radio station, and the next moment, I was being brought back to consciousness by a stranger banging on the window beside my head and yelling at me to open my door.

When I first heard his voice, he appeared to be far in the distance. As my awareness came back into my body and surroundings, his voice became louder and louder; and as I opened my eyes, I realized his face was inches away, with only a sheet of glass separating us. Repeating himself, he yelled at me to open my driver's door. He said my gas tank had erupted, and the gas was all over the road. It wasn't safe, and I had to get out of my car because it could ignite at any moment.

I had no idea who he was, what had happened, or why my car was in the middle of the intersection, facing a different direction. When I opened the car door, he reached across my body and unlatched my seat belt. He lifted me out of the driver's seat and assisted me to the passenger seat of his car, where he and his wife kept me warm and safe until the emergency crew arrived.

This accident changed everything about my life. If I had to describe my life, pre-accident, it was amazing and fulfilling! I had the career I had manifested, a wonderful marriage, two amazing sons, and an active social life. My family was large and loving, with all those unique aspects of extended family that we all appreciate and sometimes struggle with.

I was in the best physical shape of my life. I power-walked in marathons and was active with friends, family, and my community. Overall, I felt emotionally, mentally, physically, and spiritually on top of the world.

I experienced severe whiplash, as well as a concussion. Following the accident, I struggled with constant exhaustion from the physical pain that radiated throughout my body. I had trouble concentrating and retaining information. For many months it was a struggle to get out of bed, and the normal daily pleasures and chores that I took for granted prior to the accident were now a struggle. I went on to suffer from post-traumatic stress disorder (PTSD), as well as depression and fibromyalgia, and became addicted to prescription pain and anxiety medications.

Like a house made out of a deck of cards, the fallout from the accident was a complete destruction of my previous life, as what I perceived it to be, as a successful individual. I lost my job and received modest disability benefits for a brief time, and my marriage of 30 years ended. It also meant that we sold our family home and divided our possessions, and I wound up living in a one-bedroom, hole-in-the-wall basement apartment that was advertised as being furnished.

When I moved in, there was only a box spring and mattress on the floor, with a cocktail table and chair, with the owner explaining that the furniture I saw when I initially viewed the apartment, belonged to the previous tenant. I moved out as soon as I was physically able.

The fallout from this accident changed my life forever!

The Power of Empty

You see, since I was a child, I discovered we live in a multidimensional universe. As a child, I labeled this multidimensional universe as the *Spirit World*, a name that stuck with me ever since. The first thing you need to know about the Spirit World is that it is similar to a matrix, where there are no limits to what is possible, and you can manifest anything into physical reality. I had a deep connection with not only the physical world, which provides the gifts of sight, smell, touch, taste, and hearing, but also with the Spirit World.

I discovered I have the gift of telepathy, the ability to communicate with people using only my mind. Another form of mind communication includes the ability to speak with people who are no longer in a physical body. This ability is referred to as mediumship. I also see people, places, events and objects in my mind's eye, from anywhere on earth, even though I am not physically there, which is known as *remote viewing*. If I were to ask you to imagine what your shoes look like in your mind, just like a photograph, that ability is what is referred to as seeing with your mind's eye.

I am an empath, a person with the ability to perceive the mental and emotional state of another individual. I experience emotions that match another person's emotions, discerning what another person is thinking or feeling, all the while sharing in a collective consciousness, with a sense of awareness that I am connected with our planet, and everyone and everything on and around it. As an empath, I can detect the imbalances in another person's energy field, which shows up in the physical body as illness. By sending healing intention toward that energy imbalance, I discovered I can effectively assist in the body's natural healing ability.

As a result of my heightened awareness of other people's energy fields, I discovered I have a high degree of accuracy when revealing a complete stranger's current life details, as well as predicting future events they will experience, along with the best possible action they can take to enhance the experience for an optimal outcome.

Everything that happens in the universe begins with our intention. Earlier in my life, I discovered that my clear intention of thought would regularly result in my receiving exactly what I focused on, such as receiving unexpected money, finding expensive jewelry, bending time so I would not be late, and manifesting my partner and a career.

Living Supernatural in the Natural World

I learned to take the power of my clear, calm, precise intention to the next level, by manipulating the natural elements of air, water, metal, and fire, discovering they too will respond to my specific intention to change direction, shape, and intensity in the physical world.

This ability to connect in with the forces of nature is best explained by using an analogy. First, you would have to imagine that everything on this planet emits an electrical frequency, including you. Consider yourself as a human radio transmitter, transmitting your personal frequency out into the universe through your words, thoughts, and feelings, to which the universe then responds.

You are also a receiver of frequency. As an electrical frequency receiver, you have the ability to tune into and receive messages from the other transmitters, much like changing the dial on a radio to receive different radio stations. Although I knew from a very early age that I have this ability, I came to discover as I grew up that most people do not seem to know they have this ability as well!

For example, one day, when I was about seven years old, I was on the school playground in Toronto, and several of the girls were chatting about how they wished they could speak with their grandparents more often. It came about that many of the girls had grandparents who lived far away and, in those days, long distance telephone calls were expensive. This prevented them from speaking to their grandparents on a more frequent basis. I responded that I spoke with my grandmother, who lived on Canada's east coast in Nova Scotia, every day!

Astonished, they wanted to know how I was able to do that (given the cost of long distance telephone calls at that time). I responded that I spoke to her in my head every night before I went to sleep. That was how I learned that not everyone was able to use telepathy to communicate with other people!

My descent into chaos, as my world literally fell apart around me, was so severe and complete that I even lost my ability, for a time, to connect with the Spirit World. For the first time in my life, I felt truly alone!

The Power of Empty

Following the accident, for the first time in my life, I felt truly lost, and terrified! I lost the connection to myself, and the larger connection to everything and everyone that is the natural state of being known as the *Spirit World*. My recovery included rediscovering my purpose in life and my need to be true to myself and my path in this lifetime. I have discovered that this state of disconnection and sense of separateness is something that many people struggle with. It is my hope that through my life's experience you can reclaim your true spiritual heritage and learn to recognize that we are all connected and never alone!

The wake-up call from the universe was delivered in a way that shook up my entire identity and sense of who I was, up until that point. It was, in retrospect, a necessary metaphorical head shake, to have me own up to and present my true abilities and gifts to the world. It was a reminder that my role in life is to help people awaken to their personal greatness, and to become aware of their own special gifts. My purpose is to inspire and empower you to recognize the greatness that you are, and to make the world a better place.

I want to help you awaken to your true, multidimensional self and find your path on how to best serve humanity in this lifetime. I truly believe that we are spiritual beings having a human experience! This book is my introduction to your path of personal development and growth, as I believe everyone shares the spiritual heritage that I am connected to!

It was in the experience of disconnecting with the Spirit World, and then taking the actions necessary to reconnect, that gives me the confidence that I can help you discover your inner Spirit World as well.

The true-life events described in this book are my personal experiences. The purpose of sharing them is for you to view them as a jumping off point to what you are capable of. This is not my story. This is our story of what is possible.

Wishing you all the best on your path of discovery and awakening to your greater self!

Chapter 2

Change the Weather, Save Your Life

I met my partner, Jack, in 2010. In March 2011, we decided to take a trip together. At this point, we had been together just six months, but he had told me that he liked to take a trip after his busy season at the beginning of the year, and he invited me to join him. Of course, I said yes, and we decided on Hawaii, since neither one of us had been there before.

On the evening of Thursday, March 10th, we attended Oahu's Germaine's Luau. My first impression was that it was like stepping into the vintage movie, *Blue Hawaii,* starring Elvis Presley. As we walked along the designated path from the parking lot to the event, the illuminated oil-lit tiki lamps shone brightly against the night sky, revealing the grand pergola entrance to the Luau. Now on the beach, we were greeted by beautiful native women oscillating their hips, swaying their long grass skirts to and fro in perfect unison with the Hawaiian music that lingered on the breeze off the ocean just meters away.

"Aloha," they said as they placed the gently fragrant flower leis around our necks, which accompanied the rum and coconut drinks served in coconut shells with colourful mini umbrellas tucked inside.

Everything about the atmosphere and experience felt native, rugged, and elegant, all at the same time. Even the pig was roasted in the traditional way, cooked in a charcoal pit dug deep in the sand on the beach. With mouth-watering anticipation for all to see, dinner was presented as a show in itself. With horns blaring and drums pounding, they uncovered the pit, revealing the delicacy we were about to feast on.

During dinner, with our bench style seating and tables placed circularly around the stage, the audience enjoyed the entertainment of traditional singing and dancing, with the finale consisting of fire dancing from all angles. It was over the top with talented performers, and much more than I thought it would be. Following the ending of the last performance, around 10 pm, we gathered our souvenirs and boarded the bus to return to our hotel.

The tour guide then got up and, using the PA system, asked the group, "Was dinner great?" Of course, there was a lot of cheering, and calls of, "Yes, it was!" He went on and on about how great everything was as he recapped the highlights of the evening, and we all cheered in agreement. Then, he said, "Well, that was the good news. Now for the bad news." Then he shared that Japan had experienced an earthquake about eight hours earlier, and that meant a tsunami was on its way. It was expected to hit the island around 3:20 am. He then made some recommendations, including moving to higher ground. The look on his face and his tone of voice indicated that we were in trouble.

Individuals started asking for details, but the answers were less than reassuring. Did they know how high the tsunami was going to get? Did they know how high the highest peak was on the island? The atmosphere went from a great party mood to a very somber one as we contemplated the news we had just received, and its impact on the night ahead.

We were told the tsunami (tidal wave) from Japan was moving at about 100 mph and was an estimated 100 feet (or ten stories) high. It was gaining speed as it raced across the open Pacific Ocean en route to Hawaii. The date on our souvenir photo from Germaine's Luau was March 10th. The earthquake and resulting tsunami struck Japan in the afternoon of March 11th. The difference in dates is due to Hawaii being on the other side of the International Date Line from Japan.

There was a convenience store across the street from our hotel. Jack and I decided on a plan. Jack was going to take our bags from the day's outings to the hotel room, and I headed to the convenience store to get whatever emergency supplies, such as food, water, and flashlights, that I could get my hands on. Who knew when rescuers might be able to reach us, and we didn't know how long we might be without the necessities. I had a mental list in my mind, but that went out the window once I got there. When I entered the store, the staff closed and locked the doors immediately behind me, and I was the last person that was allowed into the store. There were many people stranded outside the doors, frantically trying to get in. But the owners and workers wanted to leave and get home to their own families.

There were no carts, so I grabbed multiple hand baskets and pushed them down the aisles, using my feet. The Spirit World started giving me directions for things that I needed. One such direction was to "not forget the children." I was directed to grab baby food, and even a specific size of diaper, plus a soother or pacifier. Later, the reason would be made clear to me, but at the time, I just listened and threw them in the basket.

I grabbed a couple of flashlights, some batteries, and food that was edible and required little preparation. By the time I was done, I had enough food for us to get through about a week.

After Jack dropped off our bags, he raced back across the street to help me and see how I was doing. So many people still wanted in, and it started to turn into mayhem. I started pulling off extra supplies for those individuals that couldn't get in. I intended to share whatever extra supplies I could grab, with those other people stranded outside the store.

As the manager was checking me out, he saw I had way too much to carry back on my own, so he asked if I needed help or if there was someone outside who could help me. I spotted Jack in the crowd outside the door, and said I had help. I told him that I would be okay, and if I couldn't carry it, and people needed it, then I was just going to give it to them. The manager looked at me oddly, but he just kept packing the bags. I purchased all my goods, and Jack was allowed in to help me, and then they bolted the doors of the store. I was the last one in, and I was the last one out.

By then, the crowd had dispersed, and the streets appeared to be almost deserted. Once we reached our room on the fourth floor, I started filling any containers I could find, with drinking water. Then I started storing them up on shelves, while emptying the shelves of any blankets, sheets, and pillows, to make room for those containers of drinking water. I even remember putting a container of water in the microwave, which was above my head, because I thought it would be a safe place to store drinking water, although I wasn't sure that our room wouldn't fill up with ocean water.

By this time, it was after 1 am, and we were counting down to that 3:20 am deadline. It had been a long day, including a big meal and some drinking at the Luau. Jack decided to take a nap to get some rest, in case, as he said, "I need to carry little old ladies up the stairs."

Now that I had done all I thought was physically possible, and I was satisfied that the to-do list, which had come to me like a raging fire that needed to be put out, was completed, it was now time to connect with the Spirit World and get the bigger picture of what was going on, and what I could do about it. Not believing in coincidence in any shape or form, I rejected the thought that the universe would place me in the middle of the Pacific Ocean, just to wash me off an island. There was a message in this experience, and my instincts told me I could find out what that message was by meditating. As an avid meditator, I was confident I would be able to go into a meditative state, and placed myself comfortably on the bed, beside Jack.

I was not panicking in the least! I was still receiving a list of instructions and things to do, and as long as there was a *to-do* list to do, I was good. Releasing my mind's *monkey chatter* thoughts, starting from the top of my head, I systematically worked my way down my body, releasing any tension that I came across along the way. Once the physical tension was released, I started lengthening my breath, synchronizing it down to the gentle rolling thoughts and feelings of calmness on the inhale, and peace on the exhale. This progressive relaxation method continued until the words and thoughts of my breath lingered off into the far distance of nonexistence, and my attention became captured by the flowing, cloudlike movement that appeared behind my eyelids, which I had not noticed during my breathing exercise.

Now, watching the rolling shades and shapes rotating in and out of view, I felt as though I were actually moving forward, living the experience from a bird's eye perspective. It was in this experience that I realized I had become the observer of my thoughts, as though my thoughts belonged to someone else, and I was only observing them. This is the epic sweet spot of meditation that I aspire to achieve—where my body, surroundings, and time no longer exist— the place I call *the Spirit World,* where I can observe and feel the full experience of the universe in its loving truth, simultaneously knowing that both worlds live within me and are only a thought away. While maintaining this high state of calm peaceful awareness, I brought my attention back into my body with absolute understanding and acceptance that I am an active participant to create the outcome I desired, and I thought: "Okay, I can do this."

We were staying in the Ilikai Hotel, made famous in the opening credits of the original *Hawaii Five-O* television series, from the early 1970s. The hotel in Waikiki was built around 1961, following a devastating tsunami that struck Hawaii in 1960. It was designed to withstand a tsunami strike and was in the shape of the letter Y, with the stem facing the water. The first couple of floors were open, with no windows, to resist the flow of water. If a tsunami hit the hotel, the water would flow through the hotel and out to the street in front, with minimal damage.

Over the PA system of our hotel, every 30 minutes or so, someone would give us an update on the status of the tsunami, and they would go over their protocol of what they would be doing prior to the tsunami hitting land. One of those things would be to evacuate those guests on the lower floors, to the higher floors.

There was a young man's voice that started these early warnings over the PA system, giving the higher floor numbers where each of the lower floors would evacuate to. As we got later into the evening and early morning, the young man, although trying to give words of comfort, with each announcement, his voice continued to fade and crack as he spoke with larger gaps of silence mid-sentence. It was starting to sound as if he was crying. Jack and I both looked at each other, believing he was really panicking. We realized he was on the ground floor, and he was probably wishing the PA system was on a higher floor in the hotel.

During this time, Jack and I were checking in with each other. Remember, we had only known each other for a relatively short period, and this was a high-pressure situation. We were learning how we each handled stress and dealt with intense situations, while building a deeper understanding of each other. About 2:20 am, with the tsunami about an hour away, the young man on the PA was sounding extremely panicky. It was clear he was having a meltdown on the PA system. I had an image of him lying in the fetal position on the floor! At 2:30 am, a different, older sounding male voice came over the PA system, and he started giving instructions to begin the evacuation. We were told to take certain items and leave everything else behind. Our evacuation point was the hallway of the 14th floor. When we arrived, we saw a young family with a baby. Jack saw them and said, "Huh, baby food and diapers." Up to that point, we hadn't seen any young families, but now, the instructions I had received earlier made sense.

I was still aligned with the Spirit World through this entire process, which intuitively directed me to follow a pathway that led to an area that was marked *staff only*. I was not the only one to have this idea. While meeting up with other hotel guests in these off-limit areas, there was an unspoken understanding that we were all searching for the same thing. We wanted to be able to see what was coming, not just hear about it over the PA system. So, we started looking for this balcony that I had seen in my mind's eye. Eventually, after opening a variety of doors and following a few hallways, we found this large balcony that had air conditioning units on it. The balcony had an open wrought iron rail that faced out toward the ocean and was normally used by maintenance people. As we looked up and down, we could see people were out on their balconies, throughout the hotel.

It seemed as if everyone had their televisions on and balcony doors open. We could hear CNN blaring in the background, reporting live a few miles away on our left from the dormant Diamond Head Volcano. Down below us, we could see the marina and various pathways, which were all lit up. We watched as two young men came out from the hotel and sat on a park bench, facing the ocean, waiting to watch the arrival of the tsunami from front row seats. At least that was our best guess. Security guards came out and brought them back inside, as they were facing certain death if they stayed where they were. We heard the CNN reporter interviewing an oceanographer, who noted that numerous sensors on the ocean floor were gauging the speed and direction, amongst other factors, of the approaching tsunami. The CNN reporter was in constant contact with the main research office in Hawaii that was receiving the data from the sensors. He explained that the water was going to recede, and we would see the ocean bed. Then, almost instantly, the ocean would surge back with the tsunami wave.

Jack noticed that almost the entire time we had been out on the balcony, I had put myself into a relaxed and deep meditative state while looking out to the ocean. In my mind, I was speaking with the ocean, and when I did that, I connected in with tens of thousands of other people, doing the exact same thing that I was. We were all speaking with the ocean, sending it our love, calmness, and peace, telling the ocean that it was okay, and it could rest now, thus taking some of the energy out of that tsunami.

As we watched the waters recede, we could see the boats from the marina go down and touch the sandy ocean floor. The water was completely out of our view, going further out than the lights from the marina could show. There was an extended beach where there had been no beach before, all the way to our left, as far as Diamond Head, several miles away.

We could hear the oceanographer from CNN explaining that the tsunami would come ashore any time now. It never happened! Little by little, we watched the ocean slowly come back into the marina. All the boats gently rose until they were all afloat. The water didn't come in any higher than its previous normal levels! The reporter asked the scientists what was going on. They expressed surprise by this turn of events and were puzzled by it. After all, their instruments were saying the tsunami was directly in front of the shoreline, but in reality, what we were seeing was an extremely calm ocean along the entire coastline! I smiled at Jack and continued sending the ocean the same calming energy. That large crowd, I had sensed, was doing the same thing. It was a euphoric, energetically unified feeling!

Again, the reporter asked the oceanographer for a moment to moment update as to what was taking place, to which the oceanographer announced that his instruments indicated the tsunami was directly in front of us. We saw the ocean recede for a second time, in which the oceanographer indicated the tsunami surge would follow within seconds. But just as before, it came back in, relatively calmly. The oceanographer, now in direct contact with his team at the Weather Bureau, was saying that this was unprecedented! Their instruments indicated the tsunami was bouncing between the islands while passing through on its way to pummel the U.S. west coast. The final report was that the tsunami had moved past Hawaii with heavy waves, while inflicting a modest level of property damage. One house was reportedly washed out to sea, with no lives or other property lost.

Now that the danger was past, we were given the all-clear to go back to our rooms, but there was no official explanation ever given for what had happened. We ended up donating our food purchases to a Honolulu food bank. Curious to learn more about what had happened, we talked with many locals, and it was interesting to hear their take on the situation. Those who were indigenous to the islands were quick to say, "Of course, it didn't hit us. We were talking to it." They had been doing what I had been doing during the tsunami. It was very enlightening to me to come across like-minded people with the same understanding as I had of the event, and who had a similar experience to mine.

In 2016, I was introduced to Dr. William Tiller, a physicist and engineering scientist. He retired as a tenured professor from Stanford University, in the Department of Material Science and Engineering, and was a consultant to government and industry. Dr. William Tiller has many academic achievements to his credit, including five patents. He is also the founding director of the Academy of Parapsychology and Medicine, and the Institute of Noetic Sciences. He has studied and is extremely knowledgeable about the connection between our physical and spiritual world, as indicated on his website, www.tillerinstitute.com.

"For the last four hundred years, an unstated assumption of science is that human intention cannot affect what we call 'physical reality.' Our experimental research of the past decade shows that, for today's world and under the right conditions, this assumption is no longer correct. We humans are much more than we think we are, and Psychoenergetic Science continues to expand the proof of it." – William A. Tiller

I have a friend who I had met at several conferences held in the United States that took place over the span of a few years. We always seemed to run into each other and, because we were both from Canada, we just seemed to gravitate toward each other. In 2016, I saw a documentary that featured Dr. Tiller, and I said to Jack that the Spirit World said I was supposed to hear him speak live. He mentioned that Dr. Tiller was my friend's uncle.

I called her to see if I could meet her uncle, and she was kindly able to arrange it. The meeting took place in June of 2016, at a restaurant in Scottsdale, Arizona. It turned out to be a unique experience because I was not only able to meet with him, but I was also able to hear him speak in person. We ended up talking about the tsunami of 2011, and I revealed that I had picked up on a group of other people sending the same message. He asked me what message I sent to the ocean during that time. I told him, and he said, "That was the message that I had my people send out to it." Then his face lit up in a smile, "Nice result, huh?"

This world-renowned scientist has an incredible understanding of the natural connection and communication that I am discussing throughout these chapters. Through his continued research providing validating results, he believes that we are all much more influential and connected with each other, the universe, and our environment than we have been led to believe we are, and as a result, we have a much greater influence on the world around us than we realize.

I have continued to be part of his research since then, and I am happy to be taking part in one of his studies on the oneness that we all belong to and are a part of.

This was not to be my last opportunity to connect with the weather and add my influence to that of thousands of others. Following the tsunami in 2011, I found myself on vacation in Southern Florida. In early 2016, I went to visit my dear friends, Darlene and Richard, at their winter home, in Fort Myers, Florida. One evening, while taking advantage of the calm lull between heavy rain and strong winds, Jack and I walked back from the community clubhouse to Darlene and Richard's mobile home. With no rain or wind to contend with, we stopped mid-route to watch the colourful cosmic dance of the sheet lightning that lit the sky in sporadic bursts every few seconds as far as the eye could see. The terms *sheet lightning* or *heat lightning* refer to lightning embedded within a cloud, which lights up as a sheet of luminosity during the flash. Captivated by the wide variety of colours, including lilac, white, blue, orange and red, my outward sky gazing led me to view the formations directly above my head. To my surprise, I recognized the distinct cloud movement of a tornado forming. I couldn't help but think, "Really?! I came all the way from Canada to Florida, only to be struck down by a tornado?"

I could see and feel the enormous energy system that was behind the forming tornado and the storm that was building. Touching Jack's arm to get his attention to look straight above, we stood there staring at the swirling formation that was rapidly coming together above our heads. I couldn't help but refer to *The Wizard of Oz* movie, saying: "We're not in Kansas anymore Dorothy!"

It suddenly occurred to me that despite the swift movement of the cloud formation, there was no wind at all where we were standing, and I said: "Oh, shit, we're in the eye." Jack and I quickly glanced at each other and, without uttering a word, simultaneously bolted into action, running back to the house. At that moment, the silence of the community was broken by the whaling sound of the weather alerts going off on people's cell phones all around us. When we arrived, the television was tuned to the Weather Channel, and we could see the satellite image with three red dots signifying three separate tornado formations on the screen. We could see where all the tornados were forming, and they were all above Fort Myers.

I sat on the couch, in what could only be described as a Buddha pose, and instantly went into a relaxing, meditative state, with my eyes open and fixed on the television screen. I intuitively connected and became one with the storm, and intuitively expressed a message similar to the one that I had given to the tsunami in Hawaii: one of peace, calm, and love. My intention was for the three forming funnels to release their raging energy and disperse. Everyone around me was staring intently at the screen as we watched the red dots dissipate and disappear one by one on the satellite image, until the sirens stopped, and the *all-clear* signal was given for our area. I then broke off my conscious intention with the weather system around us and got up.

Twenty minutes later, while I was getting a drink of water, the sirens started again, so I asked that the television be turned back to the program that had the satellite images of the storm. Again, I went back into a meditative state, consciously connecting my intention with the storm. Although having a visual is not necessary to receive the intended outcome, since it was so readily available, similar to 20 minutes earlier, I wanted to be able to see what was happening. Darlene's answer to my request was emphatic: "No!" I asked her again, and she responded: "No! What if it is a tornado? What do you think you can do about it? Where can you go?" Ear-piercing sirens were going off all around us, which now included Darlene and Richard's cell phones.

Being mindfully aware of the storm rage building all around us, I realized I had joined its energy. Now fuming mad, I barked at her: "I'm not going anywhere, and I don't have time to explain what I'm doing." Then, glaring into her eyes, I yelled: "Turn it on!" She did, and we could see from the satellite image that it was right over our heads, showing one massive red dot that filled the screen, indicating it was all around us and larger than the three previous tornadoes combined. Feeling the tornado's rage within myself, I realized that through my aggressive words toward Darlene, I had altered my energy, and adrenaline was now pumping through my veins as anger and rage.

Only moments earlier, my energy was in a calm, balanced state, in which I was able to draw my awareness to blend in with the previous twisters and have them follow my lead to relax and disperse. Now, with my energy coming from a similar vibration as the tornado's, I had to act quickly to get out of my head and into my heart, and the only way I knew how to do that was to go into a meditative state. With sirens blaring, gale force winds pounded the hail and rain on the roof and siding of the house; I lowered my shoulders, relaxed my body and breath, and brought my focus to the serene space within myself. Going deeper and deeper into a relaxed state, the exterior sounds of sirens, television, winds, rain, and conversation faded away from my awareness. Only silence filled my mind, and I had become an observer of my inner and outer self.

As I continued, I allowed my previous attention to my physical surroundings to fade away to a point where, although my eyes were open, the only thing I saw was the satellite image of the red dot on the television. I had released all emotional attachment to its meaning, and now viewed it as simply a red circle on a screen. Everything else in the room that was previously in my view had disappeared; it had become as though they were no longer there and, therefore, were non-existent to my awareness.

Now fully immersed, living as one moving force, I became fully engaged in the realization that I was, in fact, the tornado, and the tornado was me. Through my intentions that this tornado would not hurt anyone and having a sense of knowing that the tornado and I were one and the same, I projected the feelings and intention of peace, calm, and love. I began lowering the wind frequency, releasing the previous vibrating frenzy that had just moments earlier felt as though I were racing to get to the front of the pack, even though there was no front.

You see when rage is confronted with love? Heartfelt love—which can only be found in the calmness deep within your heart. Even if there is no apparent resolution, love wins! When rage is confronted with rage? Even if one or both of the opposing sides of rage have noble intentions of correcting a perceived wrongdoing to achieve peace and harmony, it is in the act of releasing the rage into the energy field of the universe, even if one of the opposing sides appears to win. In reality, no one except rage wins! When confronted with rage, your power is found in the ability to settle in and transform your inner rage into inner love. Understanding this to be true, I knew the only chance I had to produce a loving result, was to come from the place of love.

We saw on the news later that evening that the tornado ended up touching down about 10 miles away, in a small town, with only some minor property damage reported, and no casualties. Once the storm passed us, Darlene and I spoke, and I explained that she had misunderstood my intentions about wanting to see the live satellite image. Now that we had gone through that experience together, she had a clearer understanding of what I was doing and why I was asking for the Weather Channel to be turned on.

All of us were relieved, of course, because the storm had been very intense. I explained to her that everything is energy, and energy is alive. It cannot be stopped or destroyed, only transferred from form to form. I continued to explain how we, as living energy, can influence the environment around us, right up to the magnitude of tsunamis, tornadoes, and much more. We all have the ability to influence weather systems!

In the previous situations, I was reacting to weather systems that developed around me. The next story involves a weather situation that I was involved in creating. The location was the Peace Valley Sanctuary, in Caddo Valley, Arkansas, in November 2011. The mission of the sanctuary is *"...to support the education, spiritual awakening and nourishment of the multidimensional human potential."*

A group of people had gathered there, from around the United States and Canada, for a week-long retreat and spiritual development workshop, spearheaded by my friend, Christopher Tims, founder of The Order of the Blue Star. It was a special time energetically, as a very rare celestial alignment was to occur during the workshop.

On Thursday, November 11th, the group was asked to go outdoors and meditate around a large, beautiful, 700-year-old oak tree named Ahzahlah. It is, by reputation, an energy portal to the cosmos.

We spread ourselves out, with some members of the group sitting directly on the lawn, while others, such as myself, sat in lawn chairs. Ahzahlah was situated several hundred yards from the main lodge, and it stood out on its own as an eye catcher among the other trees sprinkled throughout the property and the tree line, which marked the property's border. It was a very calm, clear, mild, sunny morning.

Sitting in the lawn chair, I allowed my body and breathing to relax deeper and heavier into the chair. I reached a point where I felt so incredibly light and free that my thoughts and body seemed to be separating from one another.

This observation became real as I watched my spiritual body rise out of the lawn chair, and I walked straight ahead, stepped into, and moved down into the roots of the tree known as Ahzahlah. Once inside, I saw, experienced, and moved as though I were the lens of a movie camera, with the ability to narrow in and flow with the roots deep into the ground. When I arrived at the roots' deepest point, the camera lens instantly changed to a wide-angle perspective, and zoomed out to reveal how the roots of the tree had anchored and entangled themselves around and through an enormous crystal bed.

Awestruck by their beauty, I saw crystals the diameter of a 40-gallon drum, and the size of a three-seat sofa, which were sprinkled in every direction, criss-crossing each other, leading ever deeper into the ground, beyond the tree roots, and off into the distance like a gleaming crystal river. The second I had the thought that the crystals were acting as a natural amplifier and transmitter with the ability to strengthen our message and send it out to the universe, I found myself back in my body. I said to the people sitting around me, "Hey guys, guess what just happened to me?"

Living Supernatural in the Natural World

Christopher confirmed my crystal discovery, and recounted Ahzahlah's reputation as an energy portal to the cosmos, and the energy of the area was the reason he chose this location for our workshop experience.

He then led us in a meditation and chant of love to the planet and the cosmos, as the time ticked towards the 11th minute, of the 11th hour, of the 11th day, of the 11th month, of the 11th year. With the countdown to the 11th minute approaching, a group of us stood up and encircled the giant oak tree as a human ring around its broad trunk. Without a word spoken between us, we instinctively reached out to each other and joined hands. Stepping forward with the tree as our centre, we hugged and embraced the base of the tree and each other. Placing the cheek of my face gently against the bark of the tree, with one arm holding its base, and my other arm around the person beside me, I felt my body's energy levels rising with euphoric feelings of love.

Relaxing in the moment, drawing in a feeling of peace and tranquility, I felt the hair on the back of my head start to move. At first, I thought it might be the person behind me playing with my hair. When I looked back, I realized it wasn't them at all but rather a strong breeze that had started moving up from the ground, with increasing speed and force. The rustling sound of the tree foliage directly above our heads captured my attention. I raised my eyes to receive a clear view of a once gentle breeze that had now risen to what appeared to be gale force winds, accelerating up the tree to the higher branches, through the tree canopy into the atmosphere above, and forcing each layer of the massive, extending tree branches to sway violently to and fro. We tightened our grip on each other in an attempt to secure our safety, right up against the tree trunk.

Concerned for the other members of the group who had stayed out in the open, sitting on the grass and on lawn chairs, I scanned the area to see if they were safe, and was shocked to see they were still sitting within 5 meters of me and not being affected by the wind at all. A further scan of the property, looking as far as my eyes could see, revealed this intense airstream was localized to this one spot, and I was one of the members in its centre.

Within moments, a single fighter jet caught my attention as it flew overhead, followed by another, and then three more. We broke formation from under the tree, and the wind subsided as we watched the fighter jets fly off into the distance. A moment later, just as the fighter jets went out of view, we heard the roar of a low flying plane approaching. As we waited and watched the sky for it to appear, it revealed itself to be a large, black military plane, flying much slower than the fighter jets, as well as much lower to the ground.

At this point, a few employees of the Peace Valley retreat came outside and joined us to investigate the activity taking place on their property, and I recall one of them saying that nothing like that had ever happened before. She speculated the military must have been investigating the weather disturbance caused by our meditation around the tree. The violence of the wind, and the upward rush of our message of love, peace, and harmony that was broadcast to the cosmos, caught their attention, causing them to scramble the military jets; to which Christopher responded, with a wry smile and an all-knowing twinkle in his eyes, "I am not surprised."

In each of my previous weather experiences, I was physically present to witness how my connection influenced the weather and the environment around me. In September of 2017, I had a unique experience with Hurricane Irma. In this case, although I was thousands of miles away in Canada at the time, and unable to witness the power of this storm personally, my friends in Florida were.

I admit, I wasn't really following the hurricane updates; after all, there is a good reason this time of year is referred to as *hurricane season*. In Canada, they weren't relevant, since that isn't weather that we typically see. Now, if it had been a snow warning or updates on a pending blizzard, that would have caught my attention. Then, while working on my computer, I heard the words, *hurricane, Florida,* and *category 5,* in the same sentence, over the radio.

Having several friends who call Florida their home, I became curious as to what I missed. I thought, if something was going on, then my friend, Darlene, would know. She and her husband, Richard, reside in Fort Myers, several months of the year. Picking up the phone, I called her and asked if she had heard anything about a hurricane heading toward Florida. She responded: "Yes, I've been following it, and planned on calling you to see if you can do anything about it."

As she spoke, I Googled the words, *Hurricane hitting Florida*. Taking a quick glance at the weather station's predicted landfall mapped illustration, it was the vast size and magnitude that took me by surprise, and I responded by breaking out laughing, just as Darlene was asking me: "Can you do anything with it and protect my house?" Through my laughter, I asked: "Have you seen the size of this thing? It's huge!"

Darlene immediately started to back off her request, assuming that I couldn't do anything with it because it was too big. She said: "I know; I've been watching it. I get it, it's too big. It's too much to ask!" Still laughing out of control, I responded: "No, no, that's not it at all! What came in my mind was Moses. You know, the story in the Bible about him parting the seas? Right now, he's my hero! Damn right, I'm up for it; we're going biblical on this one. I am pumped; let's do it!" She said: "Really?" I said: "Absolutely, I am on it. What is your gut instinct telling you? How do you think your house is going to make out?" Darlene indicated that she thought it was going to be okay. "Good! Hang onto that image, and I'll see what I can do."

In my mind's eye, I put a protective bubble over her home, as well as over my other friends' homes, and then I went right into the energy of Hurricane Irma. I also started watching it live on CNN. They were telling their audience what was predicted to happen. It was supposed to hit Cuba first, essentially flattening that island, before picking up speed through the open waters of the Florida Keys. This would turn it from a Category 4 storm into a Category 5, as it made landfall on the western shores of Florida on the Gulf side.

I thought to myself, it doesn't have to pick up speed. I went into the cellular level of the storm and intentionally brought my awareness to it, just like I did with the tsunami and the tornado. I imagined blending myself in with that energy and started sending meditative energy of calmness and love into it. I pictured it maintaining its speed through the Florida Keys, reaching landfall south of Fort Myers, and visualized the waters parting away from the land on either side of the state, releasing its ferocious energy outward, away from shore, as it headed north through the centre of Florida.

Now the newscasters were indicating that Fort Myers was expected to get eight to ten feet of flooding. That eight to ten feet was just the rain from the storm itself, and not the waves of the water surge that would accompany it.

I thought to myself: *"No, it would be better if the water pushed away from the shore and gently returned to its regular levels, without the mass flooding."* That was exactly what happened. My friends posted photos on Facebook of a beach where the waters were supposed to be, but instead, it was nothing but sand. This happened, not only in Florida, but also around some of the islands as well. When the waters finally came back in, it wasn't with the same force, which meant that the damage and flooding wasn't as severe as predicted and reported by the media, including CNN.

(CNN) – *"Hurricane Irma's extraordinary strength has caused a seemingly unusual meteorological phenomenon: the eerie pushing of water away from shorelines in the Bahamas and the Gulf Coast of Florida."*

Jack and I watched one of the live reports from a meteorologist, at the same time as I was connected in with the hurricane. The meteorologist went on to recap what he had reported 24 hours earlier, and then drew a diagram of what had been expected to take place based on the computer-generated projection on the weather map. Then, he told us what actually happened, correcting the drawing to illustrate how it hit the Florida Keys, and then, with no viable explanation how, it veered to the right. All the information in their computer-generated projection indicated, for all intents and purposes, that it should never have done that. "For all you people out there praying, keep doing it. You are in charge," he said. He went on to mention that the Hurricane Reporting Centre was currently in the process of investigating the reason as to why their projected models were inaccurate.

He attributed it to prayer and human intervention. When my girlfriend contacted me later with photos of her home, showing a small amount of damage to the siding due to the high wind, the photos also revealed the rest of the building, carport, and golf cart were still intact. She also expressed her thanks. Along with the photos that were shared following the storm was a photo of one of her neighbours' homes, in her park, that was completely destroyed by high winds. What really inspired me to get involved and intervene was that it was brought to my attention, from my friends in Florida, that although all residents were asked to evacuate, not all the residents were able to leave. People were hard pressed to find gas and other basics. In the days leading up to Hurricane Irma reaching Florida, with less than a handful of northbound interstate highways to accommodate the residents, evacuation had become a complete gridlock. What would normally be an eight-hour travel time to exit the state, turned into a thirty-hour back-up. It was clear that my intervention, and the prayers of the masses, truly mattered, especially for the 27 million people that were impacted.

These experiences that I am sharing are meant to broaden your awareness and understanding of what is possible when we place our heartfelt intention into a visualization of our environment. Knowing what I have experienced, the possibilities of cleaning our oceans, our drinking water, our air quality, and replenishing our soil and food supply is absolutely attainable through the active power of thought, and we are only limited by the boundaries of our imagination and limiting beliefs.

Albert Einstein said: *"Reality is merely an illusion, albeit a very persistent one."*

Now, keeping that sense of connectivity in mind, let's stop and think for a moment about our North American Native ancestors, whom we've been told engaged in traditional rain dances. Is it possible they discovered and were fully aware of their ability to manipulate the weather all along?

I say: "Absolutely," and propose your answer might be found in a simple revealing exercise. The next time you experience a partially cloudy day, take the time to sit back, connect, and get creative making shapes with a cloud. Start with the easy shapes, such as making a donut or a tire, if you prefer. Then, expand to more difficult shapes. I once saw a cloud formation that looked exactly like the Province of Nova Scotia, while I was vacationing there, and I recognized how creative someone else had been. Another starting point would be to deliberately dissipate a cloud. Take it apart until the cloud entirely disappears.

Have fun, and get your creative juices going by inviting your friends and young ones to join you in a game of cloud shaping. This is just one exercise that can allow you to begin to explore your own connection and connectivity to the world in which you live, especially the weather!

Chapter 3

Meditation: The Original Social Media

Meditation is a means to calm the mind. When the mind is calm, the Spirit World can be heard!

I meditate every day, anywhere from 30–60 minutes, or more. I try to go to bed early so that I wake up naturally in the morning, quite often before sunrise. I have just awakened from the dream world, and am in a natural relaxed mind state, which is perfect for meditation. I find, by meditating first thing in the morning, it allows me to stay relaxed and clear-minded, thus making better choices throughout the day. To allow myself the full benefits of the morning meditation without disruption, I try to arrange my schedule so that I don't have to set a time limit on it. This means that I can allow the meditation to release itself naturally on its own, thus giving me ample time to fulfil my obligations for the day.

In my earlier years, through extensive observation, I came to the conclusion that there is no such thing as a coincidence. Coincidences are simply the universe's way of getting our attention, to give us messages and direction in life. As I mentioned, I meditate every day: that's 365 meditations a year that I do for myself. Even if I lower that number by 65, due to incidents, such as early morning meetings, obligations, sleeping in, or distractions, this still leaves me with 300 meditations a year, which does not include the meditative state I enter in preparation for client sessions.

Why is this significant? Because when I tell you that I saw, experienced, and went to the same mountain peak, every morning, for over a year and a half, during meditation, I want you to understand that this experience happened over 500 times. By the 500th meditation, I knew every square mile from this mountain view, intimately.

Those mountains are very unique and distinctive in their shape and appearance as the stone formations jut upwards from the desert floor. During my meditations, the mountains seem distinct for their earth tones, which are rich, and come alive on each visit. The ground seems so close that I could reach my hands down and run them through the reddish, clay-like earth. A breathtaking, brilliant orange and red glow appears when the mountains are illuminated by the rising sun, capturing my attention as though each of the peaks had a personality of their very own. There would also be a Native American Indian elder on each of those peaks, and I would be on one of the peaks as well. It is from this mountain top that I became familiar with the view of the landscape that flowed out from beneath my mountain peak, far into the distance.

Each of the Indians were dressed in various forms of native attire. All of them had faces that radiated wisdom and experience, although I would not describe any of them as old. There was a sense that, one by one, they had earned their place on these mountains and were now passing something important on to me. I did not understand what it was at the time, but all those meditations made it clear that these elders held special significance for me.

My heritage includes Canadian Native Metis Indian; so, seeing these Indians held significance for me, as I felt they had welcomed me as one of their own. The Native Indian elders claimed me as one of their own by performing a ceremony, placing me in the center of a healing circle. It was a wheel within a wheel pattern on the ground, oriented to the four directions of north, south, east, and west, outlined with local stones painted white.

Standing in the hub of the healing circle, I could see my mountain top in the near distance. They wanted me to understand that physical and spiritual realities are intertwined and are one and the same. Just as water can appear as a liquid, a solid, and as steam, I also have different appearances, as a living spirit, with one of them appearing as physical. The Native elders wanted to reinforce for me the understanding that when one realm is healed, the other is equally affected.

One day, as I was shopping near Niagara Falls, I came across a North American Indian style faux suede vest with fringes on it, dressed on a mannequin. Even though it was a vest, I recognized it as a close resemblance of the dress I was wearing in my meditations on top of the mountain. Once I made that connection, a voice in the Spirit World told me that I would need it, and so I bought it. I hung it in my closet, and it was soon forgotten.

As mentioned in the chapter, "Change the Weather, Save Your Life," while watching a documentary with Dr. William Tiller as a key speaker, I told Jack that Spirit said I was supposed to hear him speak live, and I was going to look him up and see if he would be speaking in Toronto anytime soon.

Now, when I first met Jack, he was associated with a company that hosted conferences throughout the United States. Thousands of people would attend, so they were large events. I attended at least four of these with Jack. As is often the case, you meet specific individuals, and you keep running into them again and again. Two amazing women from Toronto were two such individuals. Jack and I would continually bump into them at restaurants and entrances, or at the same conference booth. Since we were all from Canada, we easily struck up a conversation, as we had the sense that we had something in common. It turned out that they would be unexpected guides in my journey.

After attending a few of those conferences, I had the opportunity to attend a twelve-month spiritual growth tele-workshop in Toronto, with one workshop being held each month. There were approximately 10 participants scheduled to attend. As soon as I walked in the door of the first event, sitting there were the same two wonderful women that we kept bumping into at those United States conferences. As neither the conferences nor the tele-workshops had anything in common, it was one of those moments where I had to acknowledge the universe was throwing us together for a reason. A friendship developed, and that brings me back to my advising Jack that the Spirit World informed me that I was to go and hear Dr. William Tiller speak live.

That was when Jack reminded me that one of those women had mentioned she was related to Dr. Tiller. So, I phoned her, and she was gracious enough to agree to arrange a meeting with him. She just wanted to let me know that it would involve a trip to Arizona. The meeting was arranged, and Jack and I made plans to go there as a vacation, which would include a dinner with our friends and the Tillers.

Now, the trip itself was fairly spontaneous, with no prior plan or research about the area. We just decided to go and see where the universe took us. Jack had a meeting the morning of our departure, and the trip came up in conversation. One of his colleagues asked if we had any plans while we were in Sedona, and he said, "No, not really." She gave him the name of a spiritual tour guide and told Jack that we had to give him a call. When we landed in Phoenix, I looked at the slip of paper and decided to give the guide a call. All it said on the handwritten note was that the gentleman's name was Joseph.

He answered the phone, and I explained who we were and asked if he was available for a tour. Joseph said that he was, and he asked when we were coming to Sedona. I told him that we had just picked up our rental car, and I asked if he was available the next morning.

He started laughing, and said, "As a matter of fact, I just had a cancellation for tomorrow. Typically, I am booked months in advance. That's really good timing that we were both available at the same time."

Before we hung up, the three of us agreed to meet at 8:00 a.m. the next morning at our hotel, as Joseph recommended that we enjoy our tour before the heat of the day. The arrangement included Joseph picking us up at the front entrance of our hotel. We were just finishing breakfast in the hotel restaurant, which overlooked the front of the hotel, when we noticed a man had arrived and was now standing in the entrance way. Jack said he would pay the bill, and I went outside and introduced myself, letting him know that we were ready to go.

He was facing the road when I left the restaurant. When he turned to face me, I was struck by how calm and peaceful he appeared. He was dressed comfortably for the outdoors. To most people, he would almost have a hippy-like appearance. Joseph, as I was to learn, was very comfortable with nature and the elements. He loved to use metaphors, some of which even I struggled to fully understand.

He greeted me with a big smile on his face and opened his arms to give me a hug. I immediately stepped in to greet him with a hug in return. My nature is affectionate, so I generally am open to hugging anyone who offers. The day before, we hadn't given our full names, but just kept saying Jack and Diane, over and over. Yes, the song lyrics about Jack and Diane filtered through my head too. After I introduced myself, he smiled and said, "Of course you are, I'd know you anywhere!" He then told me that he had seen me in his meditations, making me easy to recognize, and he had been expecting me. That was a bit of a shock, although considering my journey through this life, I wasn't as surprised as most people would have been. Although I hadn't seen him in my meditations, there are no coincidences. If he saw me in his meditations, then I was meant to be here. I didn't know how it would relate to my own meditations until sometime later.

The tour took us around Sedona, where Joseph not only gave us some of the history of the geography, but he also gave us intuitive messages to help us on our life journey. Much of what he did was similar to the work that I do with my clients, serving as a spiritual guide and teacher. We had exciting conversations throughout our tour as we learned various details about Sedona. Eventually, he brought us to the Amitabha Stupa & Peace Park, a Buddhist temple of prayer and contemplation. Stupas are considered to be the body of the Buddha. People come from miles around, and it is a popular tourist site due to Sedona's reputation as one of the major energy vortexes on earth.

We paid our respects, then moved up the hillside on the pathways that have been worn into the ground by thousands of visitors over the years. The landscape was dramatically different than what I had experienced in Canada. The juniper bushes were tall and barren versus the short and squat bushes I was accustomed to seeing in the wild. It was breathtaking, and I was captivated in a way I had never been before.

Eventually, on one of the windy curves on the beaten path, we reached an open area of land, just to the left of us, where all the underbrush and trees had been cleared away. There, in front of us, was a large, man-made circle, within a circle, that resembled a wheel of a bike. With four lines of rocks evenly spaced, similar to the spokes of a wheel, the entire design was made from painted white rocks. Joseph informed us that this beautiful design was a Healing Circle.

**The Healing Circle in Sedona
displayed exactly as presented in my meditations.**

I was completely taken back by this layout of rocks, because it was exactly what I had seen in my morning meditations! But the surprises were just going to keep coming, as my adventure in the mountains of Sedona took a spiritual and deeply personal turn.

I had one of those *holy crap* moments, and I thought to myself: "If these are the rocks from my meditations, then the mountains should be over my right shoulder." I turned, and there they were, directly in front of me, exactly where they were supposed to be. It was obvious to Jack and Joseph that I was having some sort of an emotional moment. Joseph asked me if I was alright. Then I told him how they had been part of my meditation for almost two years. There was something about Joseph that gave me a feeling of comfort, and I quickly shared the details of the Indians and their appearance on each of the mountain peaks. In my head, as I scanned again, the Indians started to appear on each of mountain peaks, even as I was explaining the story to Joseph.

Meditation: The Original Social Media

At first, because of the shocked expression on his face, it occurred to me that Joseph may have thought I was crazy, but then he asked me if I'd read his website. I responded: "Joseph, I didn't even know you existed until yesterday. Why do you ask?"

It turns out, he is a Canadian Native Indian from the Brantford area, and just like me, had experienced the same calling from the Indian elders on the mountain peaks during his meditations. Only, he actually thought to ask for its name, and was told: "Thunder Mountain." My immediate response was to laugh and say: "Oh, my God, you're a genius! Of course, why didn't I think of that?"

Determined to find the one that he had seen in his visions, he started an internet search, and remarked on how long it took him to find it, because he couldn't believe how many mountains there are with the same name.

It was this search that eventually led him to make Sedona his home, where he now gives spiritual tours as part of his calling, from Thunder Mountain.

I asked if he would be offended if I went into this circle of stones, which is one of the rituals that I had seen and experienced in my meditation visions. Joseph confirmed what my own intuition was telling me, that I was supposed to step into the circle.

It occurred to me that the Native faux suede vest that I was instructed by the Spirit World to purchase, pack, and wear that morning, resembled the wardrobe I wore in the vision, as I stepped into the hub of the wheel. I realized that I was about to become part of the ritual I had seen over 500 times in my meditative state.

As I took my final step into the circle, I closed my eyes and allowed myself to go into a deep meditative state. My body began to feel lighter, as though it had disconnected from my thoughts. I felt an increase in my vibration as the elders left their mountain peaks one by one, and in my mind's eye, I saw them join me in the Healing Circle. They were all looking at me, not focusing on our surroundings at all.

One by one, they appeared and stood in the outer perimeter, while I stood in the center. Once they had all arrived, as in my previous meditations, they performed a Healing Ceremony. Only this time, in my mind's voice, they explained the meaning behind the ritual as they performed it. The appearance of these elders was so neutral, and their faces were very sombre in comparison to everything else surrounding us, that I realized the point was the energy and the ritual, not these elders who were part of it. The point was for me to recognize my position and their position in the larger scheme of things. It was about recognizing the power of the energy vortex of that area.

Thousands of people had been to the area, but to have reached the point of being on a peak with these elders, you had to be the best of the best. You are the person connected to this energy; the beautiful, colourful, amazing vortex that exists here. The experience was about taking my place among these individuals, by recognizing the purpose behind what was happening. It was ritualistic but clearly had a deeper meaning.

The first thing I understood was that the wheel was a reflection of my strengths and weaknesses. The circle provided direction for personal growth, taking notice of the areas out of balance and in need of attention for future discovery, with broader awareness of why I was born.

In my mind's eye, I was shown what I needed to remember from earlier teachings as a child and as an adolescent—teachings that came directly from the Spirit World. I saw myself as a child playing with my inner light, which appeared as an illuminated thread between my fingers.

One of these things I was shown was how I shared mind-to-mind conversations with my mother and grandmother, which was easier, faster, and more efficient than speaking verbal words; and how that mind-to-mind ability extended beyond the physical as I spoke to unborn children, anxious to come into physical form and experience the feeling of breathing, touching, creating, aging, emotions and, particularly, love.

I was shown a recurring childhood dream of which I was in complete control of leaving my body, flying high in the air to a variety of faraway lands consisting of lush green rainforests, deserts, tropical islands, large cities, and quaint villages. Then, from the perspective of a raindrop, I would fall from the sky, landing into the ocean, where I could breathe underwater and freely flow with the current along the coral reef, and experience a whirling dance amongst the tropical schools of fish as they swirled to and fro.

I was reminded of the first time I noticed the illuminating light of an aura around the exterior surface of people, animals, and plants, and how it's easier to see objects in the dark when viewed slightly off center, and then learning that what is seen in my mind's eye is actually there.

I was given a snapshot of what I still need to discover, explore, and learn, moving forward, and what I needed to share and teach in regard to discovering that I am, just as you are, a living particle of the universe, having a human experience, and what it means to be alive. I understood I was being held accountable, and as such, was instructed to work on myself, and work toward bringing all aspects of my life into balance, which was represented by the four equal divisions of the Healing Circle.

I was reminded of a catch phrase I often recited as a young woman and did my best to live by: *"I may not have control over the circumstance I find myself in, but I do have complete control over how I respond."*

This came as a result of being asked: "Does anyone ever make you angry?" To which I replied: "Yes." They wanted me to recognize that in reality, it is impossible for someone else to make me angry. Only I can do that. Anger is a reaction, which can be controlled. As a child, I was taught to be in control of myself, which was the seat of my power in this world.

I was then taken further into my past memories, and I was reminded of a revelation, which I intuitively knew to be true. When I was a young girl, I continuously shared with my mother: "I will understand God, and where I came from, before I die." To which she would respond: "Your grandmother used to say the same thing!"

It had been many years since I uttered those words, and I have experienced many aspects of that since then. With each experience and insight, I receive a broader understanding of exactly who we are as human beings, why we are here, and where we came from, starting with what I consider to be the most important component necessary for our survival and advancement. While you and I appear in our unique physical forms, in essence, collectively, we are part of the *One*—the one whole system consists of ourselves. We are unified as one living unit. We all belong to one evolving system; in part, I am you, and you are me. Everything I do reflects your growth, and everything you do reflects mine.

As an individual entity, when we observe a characteristic or trait in our self that lacks honor, we cannot disown it. You and I must work on self-growth, improving our self until we have grasped and perfected, bringing ourselves back into integrity with the intention of love.

Likewise, if we see a trait or character flaw in another human being, we cannot disown it either. We must find a suitable way to lovingly work on it until it is in harmony with the characteristics of love, understanding, and forgiveness, as we are perfectly connected as one living unit, as our collective selves.

To offer another human being love is to offer it to our self. Following enlightenment, peace joy and love are the strongest energy vibrations known to the universe and have the strongest repairing quality.

The earth's energy vibration is an average of the total energy vibration of each and every human on the planet. When considering your path of personal growth, you must first understand that everything you do, feel, think, and say, feeds into this oneness of living energy that we are part of.

We must learn to abandon judgment of others and ourselves. Instead, we must learn to communicate fully, meaningfully, and honestly, with the intention of peace, joy, and love at its base.

Gandhi nailed it when he said: *"You must be the change you want to see in the world."* For example, if you want peace in the world, you must learn to be peaceful. If you want love, then be loving. If you desire compassion, be compassionate.

The elders encouraged me to imagine what it would be like if not one single person had the concept of anger. Then they informed me, that's what it was like here on earth before wars and can be once again. It starts with one person at a time being accountable for their actions and reactions. During the ceremony, I observed what can only be described as a twin replica of myself standing on the mountain top, while I could also see myself in the circle.

At a certain point, it felt as if the ground had disappeared beneath my feet, and I was levitating between these two spots. I had the perspective of standing in the circle, while at the same time, standing on the mountain top, watching myself fulfill my role within the Healing Ceremony. It was a kaleidoscope of viewpoints, all coming together inside my head, yet it was clear and precise.

As the ceremony came to an end, I recognized that my initiation into this group of elders was complete. There was a welcome from the elders. I was moving to a new phase of my life's journey. As my consciousness came back into my body, I was able to feel the sun on my face. My connection with the earth, the sun, and the life that filled the planet was sharper and more intense, and I had a clear perspective of being synchronized and connected with it all. It was incredibly empowering and calming at the same time. I felt a sense of deep peace and unison with everything around me, unlike any other I had felt before.

Even as I was being honoured by them, I still saw myself in the form I am in now. I was the only female and pale-skinned person there. I represented the feminine balance, but at the same time, it was clear to me that I was a warrior of the divine feminine experience. The definition of feminine is not weak. Put a soldier up against a woman protecting her children, and I pity him. It was the beauty, power, and strength that was represented, which I was now a part of. My presence provided balance in their circle.

Still connected with the elders, I felt a great appreciation for their invitation and the means by which I was brought to see them, receiving the energy of the mountain and the power of their wisdom through the Healing Circle.

Spirit Rod can be seen over my temple and down my face.

Then I asked the Spirit World where the elders had gone, as they were no longer visible in my mind around the circle. They indicated that they were now beside a pile of rocks, about 6 feet away, and invited me to take my camera and have my picture taken with them. I asked Joseph to take pictures of Jack and me by the rock pile.

**Jack and I at the base of Thunder Mountain
with a Spirit Rod just behind me over my left shoulder.**

Meditation: The Original Social Media

The Spirit Rod to the left of Jack and me.

To understand how it would be possible to have my picture taken with the spirit elders living in another dimension, you would first need to understand what an aura is. Auras, also known as *Chi,* or *qi* in China, *Ki* in Japan, *Prana* in Hinduism and elsewhere in Indian culture, *Ruah* in Jewish culture, *Mana* in Hawaii, and *Manitou* in the culture of the indigenous peoples of Americas, just to name a few, is the ever-changing flow of a person's life force or energy flow around one's body. And for you Star Wars fans, you will recognize it as *The Force*.

When we pass over, although we leave our body behind, our aura continues to live, and can be captured in a photo, which is referred to as an *Orb*. These orbs have the capability of looking much like a translucent bubble or, in this case, the spirit elders were captured as a white beam of light dancing across the visual field around my body.

Upon sharing the photos with Dr. William Tiller, over dinner, he referred to them as *spirit rods,* and suspects we will be seeing more of them in the future. While Jack's camera did not pick them up, my camera did pick up a series of spirit rods, and so they were captured in the photos included in this chapter.

These spirit rods are considered orbs on steroids, thus indicating that I had a strong connection during the experience. At that moment, it was a visible representation of their presence from the Spirit World, and their desire to have a group photo taken to honor this special day of ritual and celebration.

Scenic view of Thunder Mountain, where the Indian elders stood on the peaks. Their presence was captured in the form of a Spirit Rod located at the top, and slightly to the right, of the center of the photo.

I knew that my life had taken a turn, and I always believe that these turns are for the better. As part of my journey, my intention is to spread my knowledge, educate you about your connection with others, and make the introduction to your freedom to explore and create the life you wish to have, and the ability to manifest it in the physical world. This education would be available through seminars, workshops, and taking individuals back to Sedona and other known energy vortex locations around the world.

Meditation: The Original Social Media

When leaving the area, the Spirit Rod can still be seen hovering beside the rock pile, to the left of where Jack and I stood in the other photos

Joseph White Wolf talked to us about several other spots we could visit in Sedona, before we said our goodbyes. One, which Jack and I were keen to follow up on, was Boynton Canyon, an electromagnetic vortex. While at the canyon, we visited the Kachina Woman, a huge stone mass that produces a feminine magnetic energy, and about a hundred yards away is the Warrior Rock, which provides a magnetic masculine energetic pull. It is similar to holding a magnet. On one end, there is the positive pull, and on the other end, there is a negative pull. The imbalance or push/pull that is constantly going on between them is enormous.

This is definitely one of the areas where someone—even a beginner to communicating with the Spirit World—can feel a gentle tingling, light-headedness, or clarity of thought moving within themselves, as they sit between these two stones. Between the two stones, there is a juniper tree that is now growing as a spiral between these magnetic poles. To picture how this tree looks in your own mind, imagine a wash cloth that you are wringing out. As you do so, you create a spiral, twisting effect on the wash cloth. That same effect was visible on the tree trunk, as it had grown in the push/pull energy of this area. I have included a close-up photo of one of the juniper tree limbs for your reference.

Swirling formation of a juniper limb, showing how it grew in the energy of a vortex

Meditation: The Original Social Media

I was guided to sit underneath that tree and meditate in a spot that was just perfect for someone to sit and enjoy the beautiful twisting art formation of this tree, between these two energy poles. There was tingling throughout my body while sitting under the tree. Closing my eyes to remove one of my body senses, my head felt totally open, as if anything above my ears was open to the universe. It was an experience that made me feel as if I had entered a place beyond time, space, and distance. I felt as though I was sitting in a doorway that connected me to everything on this planet and everything in the Spirit World.

Although my eyes were closed, I was still aware of and could see the brightness of the blazing sun on the other side of my eyelids. Suddenly, a darkness came over my eyes, as if I was no longer physically where I had been. Against this backdrop of darkness, a face popped into view. The face looked like an insect, with a nice, shiny green sheen to it, and it presented itself as having the same size face as a human. At the same time, it had no facial expression. In my mind's voice, I said hello and asked if it had a message for me. I asked it several questions, but the first response I received was that it was not able to show emotion on its face because it lacked the muscles to do so. Just as I realized it was intelligent and able to communicate through telepathy, it disappeared, and a new face appeared, similar to what we associate with aliens. The being had pale grey coloured skin, a round head with large almond shape eyes, small slits for a nose, a tiny mouth and completely lacked hair. I said hello, and again, it just stared at me. After several more questions, I finally received a message through mental telepathy, *"If you are not part of the solution, you are part of the problem."* It was not given with any emotion, one way or the other. I asked for clarity regarding the message, but I did not receive an answer, and then it left.

Now I started to come back into my physical body and became more connected to the world around me. I had no idea of time but thought I had been sitting in meditation for only a few minutes. Jack was nearby, speaking with a hiker, and I joined them. Then he said: "You had a good meditation." I said that it was a pleasant few minutes, but he indicated that over an hour had gone by. He had even called my name, but I hadn't responded.

The nice thing about this trip was that we did zero research about Sedona before we left. I just went with the intention of letting the universe lead the way, with the Spirit World acting as my tour guide. As you go through your life's journey and build your communication skills with the Spirit World that lives within and around you, it is important to be open to the guidance it provides, even if we do not always understand it at first.

Throughout these experiences, I realized that we are all connected, and the Spirit World is part of our world. Everything is connected to everything energetically.

The other reason I was in Arizona was that my meditations and messages from Spirit encouraged me to speak with Dr. William Tiller. When we met twice over a meal in the Scottsdale area, he and I discussed how we had both come to the same conclusion about human nature. He arrived at his conclusions through the application of science and research to test his theories; and me, through direct experience that the world and humans are far grander and greater than what society has been led to believe.

The author, Dr. Tiller and his wife.

Meditation: The Original Social Media

Dr. Tiller and the author.

Current observation of lonely, individualistic separation, and the lack of meaning to our existence, will convert to recognition of the power of our clear and collective thoughts and intentions, in heartfelt interrelationship and interconnectedness, and will serve as a catalyst for changes in the physical world—changes that consist of unified love, and it starts with you today.

When we let go of our limiting beliefs, living as one collective unit becomes instinctive and easier, in much the same way as Dr. William Tiller's group, the native Hawaiian healers, and I were connected with the tsunami, even though we had not met each other face to face.

Since then, I have become part of Dr. Tiller's experiments. As the founder of the Institute for Psychoenergetic Science, he is building a body of research that demonstrates how this connectivity and communication is possible.

At that dinner in Scottsdale, I received an invitation to hear him speak in Chicago, about a month later, as the keynote speaker at the Psychotronics Conference. He felt I would find value and receive insight from a scientific perspective about who we are as spiritual beings having a human experience, and from a fresh scientific perspective of the world.

I accepted his invitation. He was right; it was all that he said it would be, and more! It was incredible to be around all these individuals, researchers and scientists, who were discussing theories and having the kind of intense discussions that can best be illustrated by thinking of the scientists on the TV sitcom, *The Big Bang Theory*, with all their unique personalities. At times, it was over my head, as they used very scientific terminology, but at the same time, it was fascinating and exciting too. Here were people that were studying the very ability that I use every day. It was also interesting to see them demonstrate instruments that could measure these abilities, allowing for scientific research to occur. These instruments are based on the mind as an energy source and are able to study our mind's ability to effectively alter and influence outside forces—something that was previously believed to be impossible.

One such study, discussed at the conference, involved a random number generator—at least that is what I recall it being referred to. It was an instrument, much like the ones used for online gambling, which was set to spit out the numbers 1 and 2 in a random sequence, with no criteria on whether there would be more 1s or 2s during the experiment.

The experiment included individuals known for their highly intuitive abilities, and who were asked to focus their intention on the number (1 or 2) as instructed. The purpose of the experiment was to have the intuitives send their intention to the random number generator, and have the final results be in favor of that number as an overall percentage. This experiment has now been repeated hundreds of times in secured environments, with the results showing that the intuitives were, in fact, able to manipulate the random number generator to print out the number they focused on, beyond any mathematical probability of it being by chance.

Taking the experiment one step further, with the results of the first experiment documented and placed on an external hard drive secured in a vault, the intuitives were then asked to participate in a second phase of the experiment. They were now asked to focus their intentions on the opposite number they had first produced, with the intention of changing the outcome of the original experiment. In other words, if their focus was on the number 2 for the original experiment, with the random number generator printing out more 2s than 1s during the experiment. They were now asked to focus their intention on the hard drive in the vault, go back in time, and change the outcome to now reflect more number 1s as a higher percentage on the print out.

And they did it!

They confirmed scientifically what I've understood and experienced to be true throughout my life: that the mind can influence reality. When we let go of our limiting beliefs, and live in a high vibrational physical state, fully aware of our conscious connection beyond ourselves, then we have the ability to project and receive clear-minded focused thoughts and intentions that take place in an environment where time and distance have no bearing. When they shared their knowledge, they were not talking about me personally; they were talking about us, as the human race.

Words cannot begin to describe how excited I was that the universe put me exactly where I needed to be. The more we talked, the more questions they asked me about what I did and why I was there. They were just as excited to pick my brain, and they let me know that the questions they were asking would help them with their creativity toward their research, building their instruments, and future experiments. They are not only in the process of discovering the vast magnitude of how the human mind interacts with the world at large, they are also anxious to discover how the human mind interacts with the instruments. In effect, they are attempting to have their instruments mimic what I do naturally.

You, too, have this natural ability, but without the right tools, it can be hard to develop or even quantify this ability. As I found with the scientists, it was a discussion about the same thing, but from two completely different perspectives.

Throughout this chapter, it is clear that my meditation led me to make a number of connections, from Joseph White Wolf to Dr. William Tiller, and a number of different scientists. Where can meditation lead you? What social, spiritual, and physical connections can you make, just by letting go of the chatter in your mind and listening to your inner self? The answers could be incredible, but without a guide, it can be difficult to accomplish on your own.

I work with individuals in both private and corporate settings, and through workshops, to deepen your ability to connect with the calmer, unexplored self, introducing you to your inner power through meditation and mindful exercises. By doing so, you are allowing yourself to rekindle the strength, love, enthusiasm, and connection to your life, who you are, and where you fit in the world.

Even if you are just starting your journey into meditation, or have been enjoying its benefits for years, taking the time to do micro-bursts of mindful meditation can be key to creating a calm mind and reducing your level of stress, even as you make a deeper connection with the Spirit World.

For those of you who might be thinking: "I can't possibly manage this. I can't get my mind to quiet or shut down ever!" Here's the reality: Our minds were never meant to shut down. Even during moments when we are not physically conscious, such as when we sleep, our minds are busy, caring for our physical bodies while processing all the sensory input received throughout the day. We have dreams or daydreams, our minds can wander, and even during moments of intense concentration on the task at hand, our minds are still aware of what is happening around us, our body temperature, and so much more.

Miniature micro-bursts of mindful meditation are not about shutting down our busy minds, but it is about focusing in on what we want our minds to be busy with. This can be a way to clear our thoughts and reset after a negative or stressful experience.

Start by taking a moment to stop whatever you are doing and sit quietly. Focus on the intake of your breath for at least 10 breaths. You can stick your fingers out to keep track of the number you are on but keep your main focus on your breath. Notice how the air feels as it enters your nose and passes through your body. Is it hot or cold? Warm or dry? Recognize that you are breathing air that has been recycled many times over the past millions of years. It is alive, and it has memory. Connect with your body and notice how it feels as your chest and lungs expand with each breath, and then contract as you exhale. It is feeding our body. Imagine it going through your body and nurturing it, giving your body everything it needs to be healthy, and allowing the life force that is within us at this moment to change and grow.

Now, imagine that you are taking in calmness with each intake of a full breath of air. Then, on each full exhalation, you are sending out peace. Allow your mind to focus on this without being distracted by anything else. Should your thoughts wander, without judgment, simply bring your thoughts back to noticing your breath, repeating the words, *calm on the intake and peace on the outbreath*. Follow this process for each breath. You will have a beautiful circle of inhaling and exhaling, putting your mind into a place of caring and nurturing.

Most of us do not take the time to notice our own breath, and therefore, do not take the time to notice how often we shallow breathe, taking in short gulps of air that puts stress on our body. Our bodies inhale and exhale more than 17,000 times per day. By taking the time to bring yourself in the moment, while allowing the world to continue outside of yourself, you can calm your mind and central nervous system. You are connecting with your inner spirit, the essence of who you are. By bringing your mind to that calm place, you can grow and nurture yourself and others.

We can all benefit from this simple exercise. It can be performed as little as twice a day, or as many times as you see fit. We all have circumstances that need our attention. However, when we take a moment to be in the moment, there becomes a noticeable difference between responding with calm resolution and simply reacting. Allow your inner self to relax, so that you can respond appropriately versus something that you might regret later.

Instead of reacting, you can then have a controlled response.

See how this works for you. It is the beginning of connecting with your inner self and finding your own connection with the energy inside you.

Chapter 4

Who Says It's Impossible?

For years, many athletes tried and failed to run the mile in less than four minutes, with many people saying it was a physical impossibility. Despite, or perhaps because of, the psychological mystique surrounding the four-minute barrier, several runners in the early 1950s dedicated themselves to being the first to cross into the three-minute zone.

For more than a decade, the world record for running the mile had remained stuck at 4:01, a record set in 1945. There had been so many failed attempts by athletes to break the four-minute mile that many thought it was unbreakable, and dozens of medical journals reported that it was a physical impossibility for the human body to break through this barrier.

In 1954, British medical student, Roger Bannister, proved them wrong! He achieved international recognition by doing something no man had ever done before: hitting the finish line at the boundary-busting time of 3:59.4.

Since that time, more than 1,300 men have broken the four-minute barrier, with the current world record held by Moroccan, Hicham El Guerrouj, since 1999, when he came in at a stellar 3:43.

Living a miraculous life is available to all and is only limited by your beliefs! Early in Oprah Winfrey's career, she and her friend, Gail, had a conversation that included Gail teasing Oprah about Oprah one day having her own TV show. Oprah responded by stating this would happen when pigs fly. When news of The Oprah Show was announced, Gail surprised Oprah with a gift of a ceramic pig with wings. Oprah is a prime example of a woman who chooses to live her life outside of and beyond her limiting beliefs, and into the miraculous, where anything is possible.

Living Supernatural in the Natural World

Why is this relevant? The relevance lies in how important it is to recognize that in order to experience the miraculous life you were meant to live, just like the path of these incredible people, the first step is to let go of your perceived impossibilities and limiting boundaries. As we recall, many professional medical doctors, who studied human anatomy, told the athletes working toward breaking the four-minute mile that it was impossible.

It is in the athletes' and Oprah Winfrey's willingness to open themselves up to the possibility that something greater lived outside their perceived boundaries, more commonly known as beliefs, that allowed them to live an exceptional life beyond the ordinary.

Would you like to live a miraculous life? If so, wherever you are at this very moment is the perfect place to start!

I started living my miraculous life at a young age, setting expectations far beyond other people's beliefs of what I could accomplish. Based on what they thought it would take for me to achieve my passions and desires, I often heard the words: "You're just lucky."

In fact, I have lived most of my life experiencing what I first visualized in my mind's-eye down to the smallest detail, and then watched as the universe accommodated me by unfolding the details to make it a reality. As I experienced one creative thought after another, visualizing, creating, and experiencing what others considered to be impossible, I would extend myself beyond my last creative thought and see what else I could do.

Yes, there have been times—several times in fact—where there were large gaps between one miracle and the next. When I was finished being stagnant, I refocused and started creating once again.

One of those moments occurred when I was a domestic engineer. This may sound like a prestige job, but the truth of the matter is, this is another term for a stay-at-home mom. I worked harder at this than at any other position I have ever experienced in my life. It was far from the glitz and glamour of working in an office.

Who Says It's Impossible?

To top off my domestic engineering position, I provided administrative assistance for my husband's plumbing business, whose office was in our home. At other times, I also worked part-time as a school crossing guard during the day and worked evenings in a dry-cleaning shop called Top Hat Dry Cleaners.

This exhausting arrangement worked well for more than a decade. One evening, however, while there was a lull between customers at the dry cleaners, I decided it was time to throw in my running shoes and create a new life. This was going to be big, and I was excited to bring it into reality!

There I was, standing behind the counter at Top Hat Dry Cleaners, daydreaming: visualizing myself with groomed hair and manicured nails with matching lipstick. In my mind's-eye, I saw myself wearing nylons, high-heeled patent leather shoes, with a matching handbag, that complimented my professional office attire.

I visualized working as an executive in the largest corporation in the world, helping other people create a better life for themselves. In this position, traveling would be a requirement. I would extend my trips to include personal days to explore the far-away lands that awaited my arrival, beyond the four corners in which I currently worked.

In my opinion, this was a perfect plan! Was I qualified to be an executive, based on my experience or education? No, of course not! Don't be silly; of course, I was not qualified—not by a long shot! But why would that stop me? After all, I clearly saw it in my mind's eye, where everything is possible.

That night, I went home and drew up my resumé. The next day, I called my friend, who also happened to be my previous employer at Canon Canada, where I held a Credit and Collections position for six years. I accepted his invitation to join him for lunch, and he asked me to bring my resumé.

Later that afternoon, when I returned home, there was a message on my answering machine. He introduced himself as the office manager from Travelers Bank and Trust, explaining he had received my resumé and would like to book an interview with me at my earliest convenience. I returned his call, and we met the following day.

Excited by the flow of events, I called my friend, Roy, at Canon, and thanked him for passing along my resumé. Roy explained that earlier on the day I had called him, he was walking past his clerical staff's desk when her phone rang. Although he was not in the habit of answering her phone, at that moment he felt compelled to answer. It was her husband, Trevor, calling, and since she was not available, the two men began chatting. Trevor explained to Roy that he was in the process of interviewing for the position of collections, and he asked Roy if he knew of anyone he could recommend. Within hours of having that conversation, I called Roy, we had lunch, and Trevor had my resumé.

Within three days of that interview, I accepted the job offer and started immediately as Travelers Bank and Trust's very first mortgage debt collector. Without my prior knowledge, I discovered Travelers Bank and Trust was a division of Citigroup, the largest financial institution in the world.

The company was in the midst of expanding and would be moving their office to a new location in the near future. In the meantime, anxious to start my new adventure, Trevor and I worked out a temporary arrangement regarding where I would work until the move.

My first office was a 4x3-foot closet that held the mainframe computer for the company. It was placed chest high on a slender metal tower, tight in the corner, up against the wall. The phone was attached to the wall, slightly above my head from where I sat; there was an empty Dixie Cup cardboard box turned upside down on the floor, to hold my files, and a collapsible TV dining tray served as my desk. This is how I started living my vision!

After five months on the job, by taking a soft, compassionate collection approach with families, to bring their mortgages arrears up-to-date, I had thank you cards of appreciation from satisfied clients, lining the walls around my desk. I surpassed what was required of my collection position by the company, and I was promoted to the sales team.

When the opportunity for a management position arrived, I applied. During the interview, I was asked why, after all the years I had been in sales, I had never been salesperson of the month? After all, wouldn't I like to be recognized as a superstar in front of my peers?

I responded that he was correct; I had never reached the status of sales person of the month, and I went on to share that I thought being a superstar all depended on what criteria it was based on. When he asked me to continue, I went on to explain that when I started in the sales department, I sat in the processing department, which receives the client's file once a sale was made. Knowing both the processing department and my pay structure included an additional bonus that was based on closed business, I made it a habit to ask what I could do to help move the process along and make their job easier. This included organizing the needed documents and gathering any missing information to complete the file. Through that experience, I discovered that each member of that department followed the same step-by-step format as described in a master list that they stapled on the inside of each file and followed in sequence.

Taking a copy of that form, prior to passing the file over to the processing team, I took it upon myself to staple their master list on the inside of the file, as well as arrange all the paperwork in the file, in chronological order. I then took it one step further by making a check mark and dating each box, indicating it was in the file. I made a notation on the form of any documentation missing from the file, and explained my efforts to obtain it, in order for them to be able to follow the paper trail.

I went on to explain how I had noticed that when other members of the sales team entered the processing department and held a file above their head, asking for a volunteer to help with a file that required a speedy closing, each member of the processing team continually appeared to be busy, and no one responded. On the other hand, I also noticed that when I entered that department with a file requiring special attention, staff from that department tripped over each other to be the first to grab the file out of my hand.

When I was asked about the bonus structure, his understanding was that my motive was based on the importance of everyone making more bonus money. I assured him that was not what motivated me! I shared how my motivation was driven by our product and the pride that I felt, knowing I had helped a family consolidate all their debt, putting it into one lower manageable payment as a mortgage that I knew would get them out of debt faster, with less interest paid. I felt good about that and wanted them to experience that financial relief as quickly as possible. With a complete circle, the client, staff, and company all benefited from the transaction.

When I received notice that I had been chosen for the position, I was given the names of my worthy opponents, who I thought, and he agreed, were far more qualified than myself; and therefore, I asked what the deciding factor was in choosing me. I drew his attention to the fact that I had no practical experience in managing others, had weak computer skills, and had no formal education.

He said he was fully aware of my qualifications and had taken it upon himself to speak with each member of the processing team. He agreed with my previously mentioned observations, indicating he could teach me how to use a computer, but he could not teach anyone how to care, and he could not teach *character*.

In less than seven years from the evening I stood behind the counter at Top Hat Dry Cleaners, visually creating the life I was going to experience, I became the first Manager of Communications for Canada, with the largest financial institution in the world. I was managing a team of twelve staff, located in three satellite offices throughout Canada. The head office was in the U.S. I traveled often, with extra vacation days added on to my trips, and my husband regularly joined me.

Years later, after my car accident, and leaving Citigroup, I had an appointment with my psychotherapist, Daniel. From the onset of our first appointment, Daniel asked me, if I were to consider our time together productive, what would we have to do for me to consider the experience worthwhile? I replied that I was looking for a person with whom I could discuss my experiences, and who would help me understand human behavior. I also wanted to look at my past, understand what happened, and learn from it, and I did not want to take any of the painful emotion with me into the future. He agreed, and we began our conversations.

It took time to build a trusting relationship, but little by little, I started opening up and sharing my Spirit World experiences, entrusting him to provide me with a clearer understanding of people and relationships in this world.

Who Says It's Impossible?

With the ability to keep a straight face and not flinch an eye, Daniel is a master of acceptance and non-judgement of everything I share! One day, when it occurred to me how good he actually was at it, laughingly, I asked him if he was taught how to keep a straight face in school when he was studying for his license, and he thought that was a funny question. He laughed, indicating that yes, it was part of his curriculum. I smiled, congratulated him, and told him he was really good at it, saying: "You nailed it!"

In one session, when he asked what was new, I told him my father had visited my home since our last appointment, and had startled Jack in the process. I explained how Jack, my partner, had been putting his overnight bag in the trunk of his car when he caught sight of my father walking toward him in my driveway. Startled by his appearance, Jack ran back in the house.

Looking for clarity, Daniel apologized and said he understood my father had passed. I confirmed he had, but that did not stop my father from visiting. There was a pregnant pause, after which Daniel then replied, "Oh, that's right, you're a medium."

Admitting he had no source of reference to draw from, and it was out of his area of expertise, I assured him it was the people in the physical realm I could really use his help with.

Years passed, with him listening and providing clarity to help me understand tangled life situations and human nature.

One day, he texted his apology for the short notice, but he wanted to let me know he would have to reschedule that day's appointment. His dog had become ill and, after spending the night at the vet on intravenous, it was touch and go as to whether his dog would pull through.

Understanding completely, I told him I would send his dog healing energy, and if it was alright with him, could I have his dog's name. Daniel thanked me for my offer and told me that his dog's name was Otis, and that he would do one better and send me a picture of him.

Using Otis's photo as a means to connect in with his energy, I went into a meditative, relaxed state, and I spoke to him. I felt the weakness in his body and his struggle of living between two dimensions.

In my mind's eye, I visualized him lying on his side. Starting from the front of his face, like a fan giving a gentle breeze, I gently stroked his energy through the entire length of his body, releasing any impurities, all the while stimulating his healthy cells to reproduce.

During our time together, I asked Otis if he had a happy place, and what that looked like. In my mind's-eye, he shared a view from his perspective, of being in a car on a two-lane paved road, one single lane going in either direction. There was a large, open field to the right and a hill to the left that was covered in trees. He indicated there were lots of birds in those trees, but he was not interested in them at all! His excitement came from the field that he could run free in, that appeared to be to the right of the tree-covered hill. He showed me that he was off his leash, and he was not allowed off his leash anywhere else, but here, he was!

He showed me that he was with Daniel—just the two of them. Then he showed me how he and another dog would run free and play in the field, while Daniel spoke with a man who belonged with the other dog. This was absolutely his happiest place in the whole world—running off leash, being alone with Daniel and his friend!

The next day, I texted Daniel and asked how Otis was doing. He responded that Otis had made it through the night. Each day, I repeated my healing intention with Otis, sharing in his vision of his favorite place, and it wasn't long before I received word that Otis was doing well enough to go home.

Daniel and I rescheduled our appointment and, upon getting together, he asked me if I would help him understand my experience of giving distance healing. I described how I connected with Otis and could feel him within myself. With that connection, I cleared and balanced Otis's energy field, and shared my telepathic conversations, which included Otis showing me his favorite place and being leash-free.

Who Says It's Impossible?

For the first time, unprepared for the details I provided, Daniel looked surprised; he confirmed Otis's happy place was exactly as I described. I told him I was happy to help, and I explained how my life had been a continuous series of events, where the universe clears the way for me to be in the right place at the right time to help others.

One example of this happened the previous summer during the week of my birthday. Jack was scheduled to attend a board meeting in Vancouver, British Columbia, and he invited me to join him as a birthday gift and extended his trip to include vacation time.

Prior to our leaving Toronto, we discussed our intention to rent a car to explore the Vancouver area, which included my sharing that I felt a calling from Whistler, indicating I was supposed to visit. Jack was totally in agreement that he would like to do that as well, and the first morning of our arrival, while I continued to get ready for the day, Jack visited four rental car agencies, only to receive the same message: there were no cars available. As it turned out, cruise ships had arrived, and their passengers had reserved all the car rentals in the area. Jack was informed that the first available car would be in three days' time; hence, we would miss our opportunity to rent a car and drive to Whistler.

The first day, we explored the area on foot and by ferry. On the second day, the day Jack was scheduled to attend his all-day and evening meeting, he asked me what I was going to do with myself. With a cheesy grin, I replied that Whistler was still calling me, so I was going to rent a car and go for a drive. Knowing how hard he had tried to rent a car just the day before, and being told nothing was available, he laughed and said: "Good luck with that!"

Now on a mission to answer Whistler's calling, I grabbed a jacket and walked to the end of the hotel driveway, hung a left, and found a door marked *Rental Cars*. When I entered, the man behind the counter asked if he could help me. I responded: "Yes, you can. It's my birthday, and Whistler is calling my name. You, sir, have the privilege of renting me a car so I can answer that call." "It's your birthday?" he said. "Yes, it is," I responded.

Appreciating my enthusiasm, he asked me how much I was willing to spend on a rental. Continuing my silliness, I told him, "$77.00." He broke out laughing and asked me for my driver's license. He said: "Let me see what I can do," and he stepped into the back room. Moments later, he returned with paperwork and a key fob, indicating it was my lucky day. I asked what kind of car he found and how much it was going to cost. He said: "$77.00." I asked: "What kind of car can I get for $77.00?"

Placing the paperwork on the counter between us, he looked in my eyes with a cheesy smile, winked, and slowly slid the rental agreement toward me with a pen. He pointed to where he wanted me to sign and said: "Sign here. I promise you, you won't be disappointed! I'll even put the roof down for you!" Curious to find out what he was offering, and lucky to get anything at all, I signed, and followed him out to a sheltered carport at the side of the building, where he asked me to wait. Within moments, a brand new, fluorescent green Mustang convertible drove up, with him in the driver's seat. Stopping directly in front of me, he got out and said: "Step over here; let me show you how the roof works."

My voice echoed in the carport as I burst with excitement: "Are you kidding me? You're the best!" While passing the car keys, he smiled and said: "Happy birthday! You're going to Whistler, right?" I said: "Yes." He said: "Good; it's fresh off the lot and could use a long-distance drive." Thanking him profusely, I took a picture of the Mustang with the roof down, and texted it to Jack, with a happy face emoji and the caption: "I'm on my way."

With the windows and roof down, I drove on the edge of a mountain highway, and soaked in the most picturesque mountain views in the world! When I arrived at Whistler Village, known for its spectacular mountain peaks, glaciers, lakes, forests, and skiing, I wandered through the boutiques, and while standing at a cash register purchasing a book, I was struck with a sudden sense of urgency to not only walk, but actually run to the ticket booth at the base of Whistler mountain to purchase a peak-to-peak gondola ride ticket. When I arrived, I discovered I was one of the last of four people allowed on the ride for the day and watched as they closed the ticket booth directly behind me.

As I stood on the gondola platform, waiting for the enclosed ski lift to arrive, my attention was caught by two men and a woman, at the far end of the platform, calling to me and asking if I was alone and would I like to join them. I accepted their offer, and the four of us shared the gondola ride.

Who Says It's Impossible?

Following introductions, I discovered all three, along with another friend, named Cooper, were from Ontario, and had remained friends since attending university together. Margaret and Todd were husband and wife who continue to live in Ontario. They had arrived in Vancouver just a day or two earlier to visit their friend, Sol, who acknowledged himself with a hand shake, and Cooper, who was not with them today.

After university, Cooper moved to Whistler. Sol was the gentleman on his own that day, as his wife was unable to join them. Shortly after university, Cooper invited Sol to come out to Whistler for a ski trip. What was meant to be a brief vacation for Sol, turned into both men meeting and marrying their wives, and making Vancouver their home, continuing a lifelong skiing-buddy relationship between Sol and Cooper.

Sol continued to share how their relationship had evolved over the years. Pointing through the window of the gondola, he drew our attention to the mountains they skied over the years. In my mind, I heard a voice say: "These are my friends."

I now had two conversations going on: one in the physical realm, with Sol, Margaret, and Todd, and the other with a spirit person.

Replying to the spirit person, with my mind's voice, I asked: "Who are you?" He replied: "I'm Cooper. Will you help my friends?" So, here I was having a conversation with Cooper, from spirit, and three of his friends in the gondola. Throughout the conversation with Sol, he had been speaking of Cooper as though he were alive, and it took me a few seconds to sort out the details of what was going on. Cooper was telling me he had passed, but the three people in the cabin were speaking of him as though he were alive.

Up to this point, we had spoken freely and moved our positions throughout the cabin, taking in the spectacular view. Now seated, Sol and I found ourselves on one side of the gondola, facing each other, with Margaret and Todd on the other side.

Sol suddenly had difficulty speaking, stopping his sentence in mid-stream. His body language suddenly changed. His lips and face tightened as he leaned forward to rest his elbows on his knees, and he intertwined his fingers, clasping his hands together as he now looked down at the floor and stopped speaking. Margaret spoke up and told Sol it was going to be okay. She then spoke to me directly saying that prior to getting on the gondola, during lunch, they had received a phone call informing them their friend Cooper had passed away. I expressed my condolences and was relieved they were aware of his passing, and it cleared up my confusion.

Sol started speaking again and shared that a few days ago, Cooper had been in a single-vehicle accident, and they were not sure what initially caused it. Cooper had been driving these mountain roads for decades and, according to Sol, could have driven them blindfolded.

Cooper was on his way home when the accident occurred. He was driving on a highway in an area where the road and the cliff of the mountain were only separated by a guardrail.

The beginning of the guardrail was formed in such a way that the road side of the metal face plate, joining all the wooden posts together, began directly at ground level, increasing in height as it hugged the cliff's edge, building up to the height of a bumper of a vehicle.

For unknown reasons, Cooper's front tire of his truck caught on the beginning outer edge of the guardrail, at ground level. With the gradual increasing height of the guardrail, along with the momentum of the truck's speed, Cooper's truck rose off the pavement as it rode the guardrail. The guardrail was now acting as a ramp and flipped Cooper's truck. He had been in a coma ever since. As Sol shared the story of Cooper's accident, Cooper was chattering in my mind, wanting me to tell Sol he was okay. He wanted all of them to know he loved them, and that he had left on his own terms.

Now, I had a dilemma to solve! How do I deliver Cooper's message without overwhelming Sol, Margaret, and Todd, into feeling trapped in a gondola with me, being a medium, which could open an entirely new set of questions and issues on its own.

Empathetic to the situation, I listened to Sol as he shared his thoughts and feelings about the loss of his friend. It was when he shared that he felt Cooper had left too soon, that I took it as an opening to share Cooper's message.

Who Says It's Impossible?

I started by saying I understood how he felt, and I used to feel the same way too, about people leaving too soon, but now I don't. Now I believe we do not leave one second before we are ready! I asked him if he had ever heard stories where a sick, dying, or old person held on until after an event, or the arrival of a person they loved. I went on to say: "It happens all the time, and because it happens all the time, and I don't believe in coincidence, I've come to the conclusion we have a choice as to when we leave."

Sol responded: "It's funny you should say that. Cooper's daughter was on vacation in England when the accident happened, and the first flight she was able to get was the red-eye last night. We were just talking about that over lunch when we got the call about Cooper passing, and knowing how close Cooper and his daughter were, how nice it was that Cooper was able to hang on until she got here to say goodbye."

I acknowledged their observation and followed up with: "And that's why I don't believe your friend left one second before he was ready. With all the stories you shared about your life with Cooper, it sounds like there is a lot of love here too. After all, he waited until you arrived! I think he's telling you that he's okay, and he didn't leave one second before he was meant to!" They agreed and thanked me for the insight, while expressing how glad they were that we had run into each other on the platform and shared a gondola ride.

These experiences, which include the power of intention, healing, telepathy, and mediumship, are primary examples of what you are capable of.

Who gets to say what's possible?

Chapter 5

Continuum: When Does Life Begin or End?

When I was a little girl, lying in bed waiting to fall asleep, I would hear and have conversations with people in my mind's voice. Some of these people, such as my mother and grandmother, were living in the physical world, and some of them were not. One of those people was a little boy named Jimmy. He lived in the Spirit World, looking forward to being alive here on earth. One day, his curiosity led him to ask me about the best part of my day, and questions that helped me to give him greater detail about my physical surroundings. I was eleven years old and happy to share the highlight of my day, such as playing in my neighbor's garage with Joanne and Nancy, two sisters who were close to my age and lived two doors away.

I excitedly told him how we had lined the garage floor with plastic containers filled with the remnants of whole and crushed flower petals, picked straight out of their garden. I went on to share how each container of flower petals consisted of different flower combinations, which gave off different fragrances. When we put our slithery goo through a kitchen strainer, we were left with different shades of a beautiful translucent liquid that we pretended we were going to sell as perfume.

I described the excitement of running my hands through the flowerbeds, and how I picked and held them in my hands like a giant bouquet. Jimmy asked so many questions that prompted me to give more details about the experience. What did each of the different flowers look like? Did I count the petals as I picked them off the stem? How many petals did they have? What did they smell like? How did they feel against my skin? Did I notice if they had anything in common? If so, did it remind me of anything else?

Responding to his questions, memories of the day flooded back into my mind as I thought about each aspect of the adventure. I gave Jimmy a description of how some of the flowers had a soft peach fuzz texture on the petals, while others appeared shiny and rubbery, like the rubber on my boots. I noticed that despite the hot summer's day, the center of the flowers felt fresh and cool to the touch on the tip of my nose and my cheeks while I inhaled their fragrance. Some were fragrant, and some were not, but they all exuded a radiant translucent halo that surrounded and encompassed each one when I softened my eyes to look at them.

We talked about how it was possible that each generation of flowers knew exactly how to grow and turn into a replica of the parent flower from which the seed came, how the simple act of noticing the flower made it appear radiant, as though it had a personality of its own, and made me tingle as I felt its presence within me. I shared that although there was a common agreement between the sisters that the flowers did not have feelings, I disagreed, and felt that they did.

While counting the flower petals, I noticed a pattern of 3, 5, and 8, in the number of petals that were on each flower, and how those numbers repeated themselves in a variety of plants. I was drawn to the visual spiral and symmetry they all seemed to share in one form or another, which immediately linked me to a memory of the spiral formation of certain types of shells I picked up while beachcombing on the shores of the Atlantic Ocean, in Nova Scotia. Later in my life, I learned that this recurring spiral formation was called a Fibonacci sequence, a numerical pattern found in nature throughout the world.

After listening to how my day went, Jimmy wanted to know more about the kids who lived on my street. He was interested in hearing more stories about what we did and what it was like to join our creative thoughts together. His questions seemed to be geared toward understanding my experiences on a deeper level, which made me evaluate them in a different way as well.

We talked about the families, brothers, sisters, and cousins, all of whom lived on my street. He asked me: "What is it like to have a brother?" I had never thought about it before, and I didn't quite know how to answer at first. Once I did think about it, what came to my mind was that my brother was the first person, other than my mother, whom I had built a relationship with. My brother was the one who taught me about the concept of fair play, about taking turns, sharing, and how to be a gracious loser, as I watched him win over and over again.

It occurred to me that while enduring my brother's roughhousing, taunting, and teasing, having an older brother taught me about patience, tolerance, and forgiveness. At the same time, if anyone ever tried to harm me, he was always the first to step in on my behalf. For the times he couldn't be there, he was the perfect teacher who showed me how to stand up for myself and make my voice heard. I thought about how different we were in personality and interests, and how, at the end of each day, I thought about how important our relationship was, and that I loved him and felt loved by him.

I asked Jimmy if he had any brothers and sisters, and he said: "No, not yet, but I will. My brothers live on your street." Surprised by his answer, I asked him what he meant by that. He told me that Mrs. Jackman, our neighbor who lived next door, was going to be his mother, and her four sons were going to be his brothers. Mrs. Jackman was a good friend of my mother's, and I played with her two older sons, Gary and Carl, on a regular basis.

Jimmy said he would be coming soon, and he wanted his mother to know that when he was going to be old enough to walk on his own, he foresaw himself having an accident with the hot oven door, which was left open. Could I pass this message onto his mother, to be careful with him around the hot oven? I promised that I would pass the message along.

The next day, I told my mother the whole story. She indicated Mrs. Jackman had not mentioned having any more children and felt that Jimmy was a figment of my imagination. In my attempt to persuade her that he was real, my mother became firm and precise with her message that Mrs. Jackman was not pregnant, was not having any more children, and she did not want to hear anything more about it. But I was equally positive that Jimmy was going to be born into that family. Jimmy had told me so!

Since my mother's child-rearing approach came from a *do-not-question-her-instructions* mindset, and she had now instructed me to drop the subject, all I could do was wait for Jimmy's arrival. A short time later, we were informed there would be a new arrival to the Jackman family. I informed my mother that it was going to be a little boy, and his name was Jimmy; and I reminded her of his request. Once again, she indicated that I wasn't to speak of this anymore. However, when I asked about what will happen when Jimmy arrives, she said that if it did turn out to be Jimmy, I was to leave the matter in her hands, and I was not to mention Jimmy to anyone.

Eventually, our neighbors told us about their new little boy, who they had named Jimmy. My mother informed me that she did not tell Mrs. Jackman about the story itself, or about my talking with Jimmy while he still lived in the Spirit World, but she assured me that she had taken care of it by reminding Mrs. Jackman about the oven, and how, in a busy house, accidents can quickly happen.

Shortly after Jimmy was born, my family and I moved off the street. However, my mother's friendship with Mrs. Jackman continued. Through these visits, my mother would reassure me that Jimmy would be fine, especially as I reminded her about the topic again when Jimmy started walking. My mother and I visited often, which allowed me to feel confident that it was taken care of, as Jimmy was never burnt from the oven door.

That conversation I had with Jimmy, before his mother was pregnant with him, has stayed with me all my life, and led me to search for the answer to the question: "When does life begin or end? Or, is it a continuum? And how did he know about his name and who his family was going to be? Did he choose them, or did they choose him?"

From my side of the conversation, Jimmy spoke with the curiosity of a child, but one with more depth and wisdom that mirrored an adult's analytical mind. Jimmy spoke from the Spirit World prior to consummation and arrival in physical form. But what about the people who speak to me at the precise moment they pass from their physical body back into spirit; are they aware of the transition?

When my husband and I were in our mid-twenties, with very little money but a big desire to take a break from our responsibilities, without our children, we booked a four-day weekend getaway in the hot summer sun, with Three Buoys Houseboats, on the Trent-Severn Waterway. It was just the escape we were looking for! When the final tally was in amongst my husband's siblings and cousins, as well as a few friends who were like family, we quickly organized a group of 30 people, which was far too many for a single houseboat. Ultimately, we needed to rent three houseboats, from Three Buoys Houseboats, to accommodate the group.

We gathered at the marina and boarded the boats Friday afternoon, and were scheduled to return early afternoon on the holiday Monday.

With several members of the group taking turns manning the wheel, maneuvering these large vessels through the shallow waters, which had tree stumps, known as deadheads, and large boulders sitting just below the surface of the water, took more than one person's attention. Our daylight travels required having spotters at the front of each boat and driving tandem much of the time. Just as we thought we had traveling these waters down to a fine art, we found ourselves chomping through a pile of rocks, which resulted in a new propeller being required on one of the boats. This delayed our trip by a mere few hours, and then we were off again.

When the water depth permitted, we pulled the houseboats side by side, tied them together, and hopped from boat to boat, taking turns partying on each of the top decks. Each day, as dusk approached, we set our sights to find a small, uninhabited island on which to set anchor. Tying the boats together once again, we bunked in for the night, and partied.

All was going well until Saturday morning at 7 a.m., when I woke up and touched my husband on the arm and announced that someone had just died. I admit, his first thought had to have been, "Not this again!" After all, this wasn't the first vacation where I made this type of announcement, and there's nothing quite like a death announcement to change the mood.

Then he asked, "Are you sure? Who is it?"

I responded: "Yes, I'm sure," and admitted that, as of that moment, I did not know who it was, but that it had the feeling of being a family member. I told him I would work on getting more detail, and I went into a meditative state, checking in on the energies of our children and parents. Once I determined it was not them, I systematically checked in on the children and family members of the guests in our group.

Once I could confirm for my husband that it was none of those people, he simply said: "Okay, then we can let it go until we get back to shore." There was nothing that we could do at the moment, and his reasoning seemed sound on the surface. In those days, of course, there was no such thing as a cell phone. Still, I couldn't help but to continue to try to determine who it was, throughout the day.

Meanwhile, back at home, as phone calls started to be made, the energy of that passing became more pronounced and gave me more information regarding the details. By that evening, I could tell him that the person had died very suddenly that morning. They had been in a standing position and had passed before their body reached the floor. I could tell him that it was from his family circle, that the individual was a relative of a relative in the generation above ours, and someone who had married into the family.

That evening, we tied up to a newly discovered island and, once again, created a floating party of our own. As phone calls continued to be made at home, I was feeling the energy of those who were finding out about the passing, and it was clear that in some ways I was more connected to what was happening at home than what was happening right around me, and I was becoming more and more upset as I empathized with the sadness of their loss.

Although I did not drink alcohol in those days, I was often told I could be found by simply following the volume of my laughter, which reaches far above the activities of the room and my surrounding environment. When my sister-in-law noticed I was not my usual, happy self, she pulled me aside and said: "I know something is wrong; tell me what it is." I had already been reminded several times by my husband that if I did not have anything concrete to share, then I should not share the news at all. As a result, I was not sharing anything except with my husband, who wanted me to keep it quiet for a variety of reasons.

When my sister-in-law confronted me, I told her about my experience and what stage of this information I was at. I could tell her that it wasn't her parents or grandparents, and that I had narrowed it down to the fact that the deceased person was someone who was loved within the family, one generation up, and once removed. I also shared that all the parents of those of us on board were saddened by the loss of this individual, and they were all in contact with each other. It was our group that was out of the loop, except for my internal knowing. Then, she went to gather her siblings and cousins, telling them what I had said. After everyone had gathered, she had me systematically check in with their families, including the siblings that were not with us, and their parents. I did as I was asked and could confirm that it was not any of those individuals.

They huddled off in the corner, and then she came back and announced that it had been decided they were going to try a ship-to-shore emergency call on the short-wave radio installed on the houseboat. The plan was to see if we could receive a response to our emergency SOS, and have the recipient place a telephone call to her parents' home on our behalf and be the go-between in a conversation.

Despite countless attempts on each frequency available on the short-wave radio, all we received was silence. When it was finally decided they would give it one more try, I whispered, "Then what?" My brother-in-law, still holding the receiver of the radio in his hand, looked back over his shoulder, smiled at me and responded: "Then we go to plan B."

With all in agreement that it would be too dangerous to travel at night, imagine my surprise, as a non-drinker, to find out that their plan B was to get me drunk. Their reasoning was that since they couldn't be sad with me, they wanted to make sure that I was happy with them. I did participate, and it helped to stifle what I was picking up from home.

The next morning, as we were going through a set of locks, taking us from one lake to another, we could make a few phone calls from a landline. It was now Sunday, and many of the passengers in our group were surprised by the discovery that they were unable to reach their parents. By Sunday evening, I could share that funeral arrangements had been made, keeping them up to date on what was happening at home.

On Monday morning, with no confirmation one way or the other available, we continued the last leg of our journey. Once docked, my husband and I went to pick up our children, who had stayed at my parents for the weekend. His brothers and sister went to their parents' home to find out if what I had shared with them over the weekend had actually happened.

Upon their arrival, they received the unsettling news that the woman they knew as Aunt June had suddenly passed away Saturday morning from a brain aneurysm and had been found on her bedroom floor. Her relationship to them was as follows: their mother's sister, Aunt Norma, was married to a man named Doug; Uncle Doug's brother was Clive, and Clive was married to June. Known to everyone as Uncle Clive and Aunt June, they were part of the inner circle of the family dynamics, and a fixture at family gatherings. It was the relation that I had said it was, and she had passed away just as I had described. Although no other member of the group had picked up on Aunt June's passing, I fully believe we all can receive, observe, and be mindful of our intuitive self in which this information is accessible. As a remote empath, I often receive intuitive information from groups of people, especially if they are experiencing a singular event, such as the stroke of midnight on New Year's Eve as it unfolds throughout the globe.

Another example happened in January of 2010, while I was relaxed in the bedroom, meditating while lying down. For 20 unsettling seconds, I felt an internal rumbling within my body, and recognized it as a large earthquake below the surface of the earth. I called out to Clyde, my partner at the time, in the other room: "Did you feel that?" He said: "No." Then, I explained that somewhere on the planet, in the past few moments, there had been an earthquake, and more than a hundred thousand souls had initially passed over during the incident.

Clyde came running into the room and asked me to repeat myself. I explained that there had just been an earthquake, and the release of over a hundred thousand souls occurred as they passed over into spirit. Clyde ran back to his desk and hopped onto Twitter and started putting out a feed asking if anyone was aware of an earthquake taking place. Within moments of his inquiry, he started receiving responses back. There had been an earthquake in Haiti, moments earlier.

It was assumed that there were small villages that had been damaged but, initially, no reports of deaths. Eventually, the reports started coming in. There were cities and villages throughout the area that could not be reached right away, so the numbers that were coming in were low at first, in the single digits, but as more areas were accessed, the numbers started to grow.

Continuum: When Does Life Begin or End?

I was keeping Clyde abreast of what I was feeling and receiving from the planet, and he was receiving confirming information from his Twitter feed. Then it hit the local news via radio and television. But Twitter was Clyde's go-to for immediate news.

My connection to this rippling energy consumed my attention for the days and weeks to follow as the aftershocks added to the turmoil. We learned that the country of Haiti was devastated by the strongest earthquake to hit the island nation in more than 200 years. At a magnitude of 7.0, the earthquake occurred along a fault line that runs right through Haiti and is situated along the boundary between the Caribbean and North American plates, which are rocky slabs that cover the planet and fit together like a giant jigsaw puzzle.

These two instances, as well as the stories throughout this book, are prime examples of what is possible when consciously awake. Known throughout the world as the field, a wave, a vibration, a holograph, the living light, or the Spirit World, they all make reference to the same thing, only with a different label. If you can, imagine a physical action or mental thought as a drop of water hitting a calm lake. When that droplet of water hits and is absorbed by the surface tension of the calm lake, it is released into the water and causes a ripple effect that extends out from the point of impact. Once the energy of that ripple effect is put out into the lake, its momentum will carry on forever, and will be received and absorbed by everything in its path. When you are tuned in with the ripple, not only do you receive the true nature of the circumstance in which the ripple was generated, you can direct very specific questions to that energy ripple and receive an absolute accurate intuitive answer back. How is that possible? As in the chapter, "Change the Weather, Save Your Life," your connection is not limited to simply observing; you can, in fact, alter its state.

As I said with Aunt June, it was an instantaneous passing of information, because as soon as it happened, I was made aware of it. Those in Haiti were a large group of individuals; as soon as I felt the movement of the earth, the feeling that followed was the release of those individuals, leaving their bodies and returning to spirit.

With gratitude, I review my life experiences and, each time, find myself pushing just a little further beyond my previous beliefs. In self-reflection, I encourage you to ask yourself: "What do I believe to be true, and why is that?" Pushing beyond limiting beliefs, I believe, is the key to discovering the true essence of who you are, and what you are capable of. The key to personal growth is the releasing of limiting beliefs about what you think is possible and pushing beyond them!

During self-reflection, I continually ask myself the above question and take the opportunity to learn more about what I am capable of and what is possible. One such opportunity came in the form of being told that the longer a person had passed, the less likely it would be that they could communicate with us, and I was excited to have the opportunity to test that theory.

In 2016, my friend, Bob, started telling me about his grandfather's brother, Captain Ed McConkey, who was the youngest captain on the Great Lakes during his time. Captain McConkey went down with his ship in the great storm of 1913. When his body was found washed up on shore, he still had his personal diary and a gold pocket watch on him, in his jacket pocket.

Bob went on to share that over the years, historians had gone to great lengths to compile the sequence of events that took place leading up to the great storm, along with the vessels that capsized, and the men who lost their lives. Although they were confident in the information they collected, there were still a lot of unanswered questions in relation to what actually happened out on the waters that day: how did it come about that a ship's crewmember, from another vessel, washed ashore, wearing a safety vest that belonged to the S.S. Regina, which was his great-uncle's boat?

Then, Bob shared that these artifacts were on display as an exhibit at the Huron County Museum, in Goderich, Ontario. The conversation took a turn, however, when he asked me to see if I could connect with his great-uncle. Then, he asked me to do a day trip to the museum, and try to connect with him, because there were still questions about that storm and some of the decisions that had been made by Captain McConkey. So, not only was there family significance for Bob, but some historical significance as well.

His offer took me completely by surprise, as Bob had never shown any interest in my abilities prior to this. I quickly agreed and asked him to refrain from sharing any more details, as I preferred to let Captain McConkey provide the missing information. Now, trying to formulate in my mind how I was going to do this, I was quick to point out that there would be a vast amount of energy associated with the tens of thousands of items in the museum.

Those other relics, and the energy associated with each one of them, would mean I would have to do some micro-filtering to find and connect with Captain McConkey. This was just one area that might be an issue if I was to give it my full attention and focus. The other concern was that I had never spoken to someone who had been deceased for over one hundred years. Other mediums had given me the impression that, as time went on, in their experience, these energies start to subside and calm down, making them harder to connect with. The more I thought about it, the more excited I became to find out if it was possible to speak with Captain McConkey under these conditions. When I shared these thoughts with Bob, I am sure he perceived them as justifications as to why I would fail, but he graciously responded: "There is no pressure. If it doesn't work out, that's fine. It will be a great road trip just the same!"

Again, thinking out loud, I made a reference to what I thought would be to our advantage: that to be a captain of an ocean liner, he would have to have been an excellent communicator. That is what gave me the interest to test my theory that this man would still be an excellent communicator, if I could make a connection with him.

I was excited to put it to the test, and I asked what the chances might be to get close to the Captain's personal diary and pocket watch that had been on his body. I thought it might help me to connect with his energy, as well as help me to filter out the other energies present in the museum.

The ability to receive information about people or events associated with an object, solely by touching or being near to it, is referred to as psychometry. I discovered early in my life that I have this ability. Science confirms everything is energy, and energy is alive. While it does change form, it never ends, nor can it ever be destroyed.

We called the museum in advance and spoke to the person on hand who oversaw the museum artifacts. Because of Bob being family, they were willing to entertain our request, but they wanted to know why we wanted to get close to the Captain's personal effects. I explained that I was an intuitive medium and that being close to the artifacts would help me to better connect with Captain McConkey's energy, and that we were hoping to answer some of the unresolved questions about what transpired the day of the great storm.

She agreed, thinking it would be an interesting experiment, but also let us know that she would have to stay with the exhibit if the artifacts were exposed. I would be within one plexiglass layer of the items, which was as close as I was going to get without touching them.

Upon our arrival, Bob and I were greeted by the staff member we had spoken to on the phone days earlier. Her intention was to lead and escort us to the exhibit, but instead, I found myself walking vigorously through the museum, leaving them behind as I followed Captain McConkey's energy. Although I had never had the privilege of going to Goderich, or to the museum, prior to this visit, I walked with purpose, directly to his display cabinet.

With keys in hand to open the plexiglass cabinet, the employee removed the larger, exterior plexiglass casing in which the diary and pocket watch were housed, allowing me to place my hands gently on either side of Captain McConkey's personal belongings. They were protected by another tight fitting, molded casing to prevent direct contact.

Diane Wargalla with Captain McConkey's pocket watch and personal diary.

Continuum: When Does Life Begin or End?

Bob McConkey and Diane Wargalla at Huron County Museum with Captain McConkey's pocket watch and diary.

Now connected with the Captain, he was excited—not only to meet me but also to meet and answer questions from his great-nephew. This experience lasted for over an hour, as I spoke on his behalf and relayed information to Bob and the very curious employee, who had now pulled up a chair and made herself comfortable, and within earshot.

The main questions that we asked related to the sinking of his ship. Much of the evidence was contradictory, and there were questions about why he had done certain things, which historians believed had contributed to the sinking of his ship.

As the conversation started, Captain McConkey shared details about his life and, particularly, details about his wife, including her brown, shoulder-length curly hair, slender body, and fair skin. It was clear that he adored her, and his love for her was only second to his love of the sea. He referred to her by a short name that started with the letter M, had 4–5 letters in it, and ended in the letter Y, which I could not make out. She was the last thing he thought of when he passed.

He also made comments to Bob, that Bob had a typical McConkey nose. Bob had not known many members of his family and had not met them as a child or seen photos, so he had no frame of reference when this comment was made.

Following this experience, the staff member in attendance provided Bob with photographs from their archives, provided by Captain McConkey's daughter when she was purging and downsizing her family's Estate. Amongst the pictures was a snapshot of Captain McConkey and his wife, Amanda (a.k.a. Mandy), in a convertible car, which revealed her fair complexion, slender frame, and long, curly dark hair, fully extending to the outer brim of the stylish hat she was wearing.

Also, among the photos, was one of Captain McConkey with his three brothers. Upon examination of all four faces, we shared a laugh when Bob recognized his nose, in the photograph, on one of his great- uncle's faces, confirming he had a classic McConkey nose.

Bob, already knowing the answer, asked Captain McConkey if there was anyone on board that he might have been related to. Bob's great-uncle, Ed, shared that there was a man on board that he was related to. The man was similar in age and someone he was very close to. I determined that it had a brother energy associated to it, in which I stated to Bob that this relationship could include a brother, brother-in-law, or close cousin. In my mind's eye, Captain McConkey showed me the moment his family member was swept overboard: one second, he was there, and then he was not. Along with this image, I also felt Captain McConkey's heartache when he witnessed this brother energy being swept overboard, prior to his own passing.

I also learned that they had passengers on board from time to time. Some of them were scheduled in advance through the proper channels, while others were actually smuggled on board, being picked up during their cargo runs, thus giving them safe passage. He made mention that there were the *rules*, and then there were the *other rules*.

Continuum: When Does Life Begin or End?

The Captain went on to tell me how he and his crew had attempted to assist another cruise ship during the storm, with the intention of rescuing members of their crew by bringing them aboard. Captain McConkey confirmed that life vests had been thrown out to those men whose cruise ship was going down, in an attempt to rescue them. He said it was a one-in-a-million shot that the life jackets would hit their target, but they had to try.

During these tense moments, fighting against the elements to reach those individuals whose ship was going down, a third ship appeared. Pirates were now on the scene, demanding that he put down his anchor. Their plan was to steal the cargo from the S.S. Regina, despite the storm. His crew was shot at as the pirates boarded the ship. At gunpoint, the demand to lower the anchor was made, and the Captain reluctantly complied. He wanted to save his men and ship, which the pirates did not care about. The pirates only wanted the cargo and cared little for the lives that could be lost.

At this point, I learned from Captain McConkey that, under normal conditions, he would never have dropped anchor. Dropping anchor during a storm puts the boat in grave danger, as water can come over the front or from the side and capsize the vessel. To maneuver properly, they needed to maintain control, riding the seas at a 45-degree angle to the waves, which was crucial to their survival and ability to ride out the storm.

What was the cargo that the pirates were so determined to obtain, and were willing to kill, and lose their lives over? Captain McConkey informed me it was whiskey, which was more valuable than gold at that point in history. There had also been gold aboard the boat, according to the logbooks, and the gold was taken by the pirates as well.

The S.S. Regina took on a wave on the starboard side. I told him I didn't understand what that meant; so, in my mind's eye, he showed me that they received a hit on the front, left side of the boat. It was a massive wave that took them down. He indicated they had already lost their rudder by that point. When I told him: "I don't know what a rudder is," he indicated they had lost control of the ship. I suddenly felt myself transported back to 1913, and in my mind's eye, saw the deck of the ship from his perspective that day, rolling out of control, which made me feel nauseous. All the decisions he made back then were to preserve lives and attempt to keep his ship safe, but ultimately, the demands of the pirates brought his ship down.

As I relayed these details, the museum employee was captivated by the details about that day, and in the process, took mental note of what was being revealed by Captain McConkey. Once finished, and with the plexiglass cabinet put back together, she shared some collaborating details from the museum archives that we did not know beforehand.

We also took the time to watch a documentary there in the museum. At first, we were anxious to get back on the road, but she said it would be worth our while to watch the film, and we finally agreed to stay for the private viewing she arranged. It was amazing and mind-blowing to see what I had learned from Captain McConkey in the Spirit World being confirmed in the physical world.

These are the types of verifiable experiences that have helped me to understand that everything that has taken place in the past, is taking place at this very moment; and everything that is currently on track to happen, is in fact occurring simultaneously, and we interpret it happening in linear form, simply to perceive it. Through my experiences and observations, I have determined that time is not linear.

Captain McConkey could answer Bob's questions and show me in great detail about his life and what occurred that day during the great storm of 1913. He could show me in real time, as if I had been there and experienced it all myself at that very moment. Jimmy spoke to me from the Spirit World prior to conception, and introduced me to his upcoming family, which he was born into.

I hope you understand through these stories that I have shared, if I can access this reality that is still running through the memory of the universe, then you can access it as well. My message is that we are profoundly connected as one living energy, and we need to honor ourselves as such. You have far more abilities than what you have ever been led to believe.

You can make a positive difference in the world, starting right now!

Continuum: When Does Life Begin or End?

We live in a beautiful time, when the sum of all human knowledge is now so immense that even a highly educated person, at the height of their utmost extreme learning capacity, can only hope to absorb a tiny bit of it.

Would you like to discover it for yourself—discover your authentic self, and the ability to change your life, and the world, for the better? Imagine falling asleep each night knowing all was well within your life and the world, knowing you created it! Imagine waking up energized, healthy, fit, bursting with excitement to start your day. What would you do? What would that look like? How would it feel?

If you and I were to meet here today, exactly three years from today, what would have had to have happened in your personal and professional life, for you to be living your ultimate dream life as a reality?

You can have those things, and much more!

Let us connect, learn from one another, and grow. Let's explore who we are and what we are capable of to our fullest capacity. Enlightenment isn't out there; enlightenment is within! Everybody is an expert at something! My expertise is living authentically and completely intertwined with my inner light, while at the same time, creatively manifesting the world that appears physical, and I would love for you to experience this limitless freedom as well.

To quote two great scientists:

"Everyone you will ever meet knows something you don't." – Bill Nye

"The world, as we have created it, is a process of our thinking. It cannot be changed without changing our thinking." – Albert Einstein

Chapter 6

Now You See Me, Now You Don't

I was twelve years old and sitting in a waiting room, while my mother talked to the therapist. It was so quiet, you could hear an ant walk across the floor. The furniture was dark and oversized, and the seat was hard around the edges, while being soft and sunken in the middle. Sitting completely back in the seat, my legs stuck straight out in front of me. Trying to get comfortable, I tucked my feet up under my bottom, which made me sink in the middle, and I fought with the arms of the chair as I wiggled out of the hole. So, there I was, sitting on the edge of the seat, swinging my feet back and forth while entertaining myself by stretching one leg to touch the floor with the flat of my shoe, with the challenge of not having my bottom slide off the rim of the chair. My Uncle Leon arrived after my mother was called in to speak to the therapist in the other room, which made me feel better because I loved being with him. He entered the room and quietly sat across from me to keep me company. He was an adult I trusted, and one who did not treat me like a kid.

I had only been told we had an appointment, and I was going to miss half a day of school. That first visit, I had no idea who the man in the other room with my mother was, why I was there, or why they felt it necessary to leave me in the waiting room. It was as though they had a secret, and I was not allowed in on it. I didn't mean to eavesdrop. I didn't even need to get off my chair, but the door between us was so thin, the whisper of their voices was the only things I could hear. Much of what they said was muddled, but what I did overhear was my mother say my name, and what she and I had been talking about these past few months.

When the door opened, the therapist invited me to join them. I felt as though I were in trouble. They both stared at me, and the therapist started asking questions about school, friends, and the changes in my life over the past few months. He said he understood that what was supposed to be a joyful time in my life had turned tragic, and no one, not even my favorite uncle, could explain why.

It all started two months before my twelfth birthday. It was an exciting time for my family! We were getting ready to celebrate the wedding of my Uncle Leon. He was in his early twenties and was more like a big brother than an uncle. I had never been to a wedding before, so this was something I had been looking forward to ever since it was announced. My mom's best friend, Marion, was his fiancée. She had a little boy, Kenny, who had not known his biological father, so my Uncle Leon had stepped into those shoes and became Daddy. Kenny was so cute that Leon could not help but fall in love with him. Kenny was ten years younger than me, and I thought of him as a little brother. As the wedding day approached, I heard they arranged to have Kenny's adoption papers drawn up and delivered to the church, where they would be signed along with the marriage certificate, and Uncle Leon would officially be Kenny's Dad. People who I had known and loved for years were about to join my family. To say I was excited was an understatement!

As we counted down to the big day, the buzzing excitement revved up and rang through the house. Our family was excited to make official this newest addition to our family. I was excited because it was not every day that I got a new dress and new shoes—it was like I was a princess planning for the ball. I remember hanging the dress on the outside of my closet door, with my shoes directly underneath, so they were the last thing I saw at night while I was counting down how many *sleeps* were left before the wedding. I was almost twelve, and everything about this wedding was a big deal to me. My mother was helping to organize the wedding and was a force to be reckoned with when it came to getting things done in our family. Naturally, she was making sure all the last-minute details were being handled. With all the comings and goings of all the people and food, you would have thought we had opened a catering business.

When it came to the night before the wedding, I wanted to go to bed early to make it happen faster. Just as I was going to bed, Uncle Leon came over with Marion's brother to say hi. He also wanted to make sure everything was ready for the next day.

Now You See Me, Now You Don't

I had never seen him so happy. He was twenty-three years old and smiled all the time. Uncle Leon was always at our house and had even started teaching me to play guitar. I don't think I really wanted to learn, but with him, I did. I was allowed to stay up while they visited, and when we walked him to the door, Uncle Leon said that he was going to spend the night with Marion's brother.

Hugging is something we do at the door, so it was not unusual for Mom and Uncle Leon to hug as he was leaving. Only this time, my mom hung on longer than usual. She hung on so long that he finally started laughing, and said, "I love you, sis; you can let go now." Releasing her hold, she told him that she loved him too. Heading out the door, he said, "Don't worry, sis. It's all good. I'm not even going to drink tonight. See you in the morning."

We stood in the open doorway waving goodbye and watched until their tail lights faded out of sight. When I glanced at my mom as she was closing the door, I noticed her eyes were welling up with tears. I asked her what was wrong and, forcing a smile, she said: "Nothing is wrong. Go to bed; we have a busy day tomorrow." What she did not share was that she knew something that would alter our family forever.

Later that night, I was startled out of a deep sleep by the sound of the phone ringing. My bed was beside the window, and I quickly glanced out to find it was still dark. The phone did not have a chance to ring twice, when I heard my mom say, "Hello."

She was quiet at first, whispering, and then taking the call down in the living room. I could not make out what she was saying at first, but the more words she said, the louder she got. I heard her clearly say, "No! Not in the morning; go wake her up now. She needs to know now! I'll stay on the phone while you go get her!"

At that point, I was out of bed, determined to find out what was going on. I was not the only one awake; the whole house was now up, and the lights were blazing. When I entered the living room doorway, my mom put her hand up like a wall, indicating that I was not to come any closer. "Go to your room. I'll be there when I'm done."

She stayed on the phone for a long time, and I could hear her talking with my father and my older brother, and the out-of-town relatives that were staying with us for the wedding. But I was not able to hear what they were talking about.

Finally, after what seemed like the longest wait in my life, I heard her come up the stairs, and then she entered my bedroom. I remember her next words as though they were just spoken yesterday. "That was Marion's brother on the phone. There has been an accident."

I do not remember anything after she said that Uncle Leon had died, but later, I learned the whole story about how it happened.

Uncle Leon and Marion's brother were on the way home at 2:00 a.m., when they came across a car that was stopped at the side of the road. The driver's door was open, and the driver was slumped over the steering wheel. He looked like he was in trouble, so Uncle Leon stopped to help.

While he was standing on the inside of the open driver's door, assisting the unconscious driver slumped in his seat, a speeding car came racing by, hitting Leon and the open door at the same time. The car door was ripped off the doorframe, and Leon was lifted up and carried on the hood of the car that hit him, until it slammed into the tail end of another parked car, further down the road.

Leon was literally lifted out of his shoes, and they lay on the road where he'd been hit, but they had trouble finding Leon himself for the longest time. When his body was located, using tracking dogs, it was determined that the car, on which he was riding on the hood of, had hit the parked car, and it had popped the trunk of the parked car. His body slid inside, and the trunk lid closed, making it difficult to locate him without the dogs.

He was killed by a drunk driver, twelve hours before his wedding and the adoption of his precious little boy, Kenny. The coroner's report confirmed that Leon had no alcohol in his system, and the official cause of death was from an artery dislocating from his heart upon impact. The driver of the car that hit him was found guilty of drunk driving, causing death.

Now You See Me, Now You Don't

This was before the computer age, so with one telephone and a few extensions, family members took turns canceling the caterer, the church, the florist, and tuxedo rentals. Plus, there were friends and family, who were not going to be attending the wedding, to be notified about Uncle Leon's death. Our family was large, with Uncle Leon being the youngest male of twelve children. With his sister, Rosalyn, passing as an infant, the surviving ten siblings were now healthy adults with families of their own, who had been looking forward to a celebration, not a funeral service.

News of his passing spread like wildfire, and even made it as a leading story on the television news and local newspapers. The phone seemed to ring incessantly. Kenny, being only twenty-two months old at the time, saw Uncle Leon in the casket and tried to climb in with his Dad, who he thought was just sleeping.

It was a living nightmare, and I couldn't wake up. Marion was on suicide watch, and the lights stayed on in the house twenty-four hours a day, for days at a time. There was always someone sitting at the kitchen table with a pot of tea on the back burner of the stove, and people came and went as if our home had a revolving door.

During this time, Mom took me everywhere she went, and seldom said where we were going. She just told me to get in the car, which I did without question. One day, as we got closer to the funeral, out of the corner of my eye, I noticed a man sitting on a bench at a bus stop. He looked just like Uncle Leon. It startled me, but when I took a second look, he was gone. This kept happening over and over again, each time in a different place, with him doing different things. I even saw him at his own funeral, sitting in a chair, studying the people in the room like a spectator.

Those first few times, he did not look at me at all. He was simply present in the background. Of course, I was catching him out of the corner of my eye, and when I turned for a second look, he would be gone.

Later, while I was sitting with my mom in the car at a red light, I was drawn to the image of a man, in the parking lot on the corner of the street, walking straight toward us. The man was about fifty feet away, and the way he walked caught my attention. Then he looked at me and smiled. It was Uncle Leon!

I did not want to blink, afraid that he would disappear. In my mind's voice, I kept telling him to hurry, being sure that if he got close enough, my mother would see him too! But then the light turned green, and we pulled away from the intersection. Until that moment, Mom and I had been sitting quietly in the car. Now, she wanted me to sit properly in my seat, because I was completely turned around and looking out the back window, and I wanted her to see Uncle Leon.

When she finally heard what I was saying, she told me she would never be able to see him, and that I shouldn't either. She told me to say a prayer for him. I was to pray that he finds easy passage into heaven, along with a prayer for myself to not see him anymore. I told her that I felt as though Uncle Leon was coming to us for a reason, and I was determined to find out what that reason was.

Thus began my trips to the therapist. Mom and I would sit on the dark, heavy leather furniture, where she expected me to be quiet and to sit still. Eventually, an older man would come out to ask my mom to step into his office—more waiting for me, and also some eavesdropping. Even with the door closed, I discovered that when I sat in the seat next to the door, I could hear everything they said. My mom told him about Uncle Leon's death, how close we were, and the impact it was having on our family, and my visions of him. The therapist referred to it as a *trauma*.

Then, it was my turn, where I spent time answering a lot of questions about school, my friends and family, as well as my sleeping habits. But his primary focus was on my sightings of Uncle Leon. For a man who was always asking about my feelings, he clearly could not observe that I felt trapped, as if I was a prisoner being held against my will. I hated going to his office. I would get knots in my stomach just at the thought of it. The more I went, the less I had to say. It was a very confusing time for me.

In the waiting room, while I was left alone, Uncle Leon would sometimes appear and sit across from me. His calm presence helped me to feel as if everything was going to be okay. One day, I told him, "I'm here because of you, you know. Because I can see you."

Then, for the first time, he spoke! He said: "If you tell them you don't see me anymore, you won't have to come back." I thought about it for a second and responded: "But that would be a lie." He said: "It doesn't have to be a lie; watch this." Then, he disappeared from sitting in the chair across from of me, and popped into my head, and said: "How's this? Better?" Startled, and excited by his actions, I burst out laughing. I spoke to him through my thoughts, and said: "Yes, a lot better; thank you!" Just then, the door to the office opened, and I was invited in. When I was asked about my Uncle sightings, since my last appointment, I told them that I did not see him anymore and continued telling them that until the therapist visits stopped.

This, according to my mother, was going to be the last of my spirit sightings, communication, and discussions on the topic. After sharing my Uncle sightings with her, and seeing the commotion it created, I thought it would be best to not talk about it for a while and took the time to get a better perspective on my metaphysical reality that seemed to stand out as different from the average person's experience of life.

One such area was my ability to hear the specific thoughts of other people at the precise moment they had them. This was mostly in relation to my mother, and I found myself in trouble on more than one occasion when I responded to her thoughts that had not yet been spoken. To adapt, I learned to watch people's lips as they spoke, in order for me to recognize the difference between receiving information through my physical realm, as opposed to information coming through direct mind-to-mind communication.

I became a teenager and could not understand why this entire section of my life was to be kept quiet. I was determined to bring up the discussion with my mother once again. I was young and did not realize that not everyone is ready or willing to have these types of discussions. This was especially true of my mother. She was definitely not ready to hear that I had discovered she had experienced a vision prior to Uncle Leon's wedding—a vision that told her he would not make it to the altar. I now understood that was why she hung onto him so tightly that last time they said goodbye.

She was furious with me and shouted: "I told you to stop doing that!" She insisted that I was forbidden to connect with the Spirit World. I told her it would be impossible for me to stop! What she was asking me to do would be the same as her asking me to change the colour of my eyes. I could not turn it on and off like a light switch—it's not one or the other—spirit and physical are the same; this is who I am!

Now, this was against all that we believed in our religious faith, so the next person she took me to speak with was the priest. According to my mom, when she spoke to the priest about me communicating with the afterlife, she had been told it was a sin against God, and it was the Devil's work. From my experience, that was the furthest from the truth that anyone could have ever told me. I am God's child, and if I was not meant to speak with the afterlife, then I would not have been born with this ability! All our gifts are meant to help and be of service to others. She held firm to her belief, and I held firm to mine.

Discussions turned into heated arguments, and appointments with the priest were short-lived, as I do not believe he wanted to have these discussions with me either. The priest finally told my mother that my coming to speak with him should not be forced. Once again, I stopped talking about my Uncle altogether, even though I was still communicating with him.

In those moments of my determination, I did not realize how much my mother was hurting. Now, although I still communicate with various loved ones who have passed on, I let people tell me if they are ready to receive the messages their loved ones have sent. I do not try to make them listen, because for some, they are simply not in a place where they can accept the content and emotion of those messages.

Communication with the Spirit World is possible for anyone, but most of us do not exercise it because we do not know what muscles to use, so to speak. Start with the knowledge that there is no such thing as a coincidence and accept it as the universe speaking to you! The coincidences are waking us up, showing us that the energy is real. Pay attention to synchronicities and hunches, and step into the flow of the universe by following the direction in which they lead. When your instincts tell you something, follow up on them! Acknowledge what you see and what you experience.

When I first saw Uncle Leon, I did a double take. My eyes were telling me something that I was sure could not be possible. He was deceased, after all.

But my heart accepted what my mind took a while to come to terms with: that Uncle Leon was contacting me.

In order for a deceased loved one to visit you, a great deal of energy must be expended to let their presence be known in our physical realm. Shifting their energetic vibration to materialize a likeness of themselves, or to speak, levitate, move and remove objects, or affect lights, electrical appliances, and radio frequencies, takes effort. Our deceased loved ones and pets are able to change their frequency vibration, give us messages, and show us that they are alive and flourishing, by providing a visual image of themselves. Whether it is during wake or sleep hours, this visual typically comes to us during a time of calmness. This visual of our loved ones' presence can also come in a form that resembles flashes of particles of light, appearing and disappearing in the forefront or in the corner of our eyes. Spirits often present themselves through symbolic messages that are relevant to them, or your relationship, and that you will recognize.

During the calmness of meditation or sleep, we lower our conscious intellectual guard of what we believe to be real and enter an altered state of consciousness where we are much more relaxed, creative, and open to receive contact from the Spirit World. Whether you are in a dream state or on the astral planes, during meditation and relaxation, these are the realms that provide the biggest impact. No matter which form your loved one is able to communicate through, in your mind's voice, speak to them. Let them know their efforts are being acknowledged and encourage them to reach out to you in other recognizable ways.

What if you are the type of person who does not typically remember your dreams? This may be as a result of a self-induced blockage that you may not even be aware of. This unconscious obstruction may be restraining your realization that you, too, greet the departed during dreamtime, and have the ability to remember the experience. Do you wish to remove this blockage and remember these visits? You could start by writing an affirmation of your intent to remember your dreams, allowing spirit to visit. You would say this affirmation each night prior to going to bed and include your intention to wake up in the morning feeling happy, refreshed, and remembering your dreams.

As the visions start, it is important to try to quiet your mind and simply witness and feel the experience for what it is: love at its finest. Unfortunately, as we saw with my Uncle Leon sightings, it is not always the case that spirit sightings will be in a quiet place away from the world. Therefore, you need to practice quieting your mind on a regular basis, making it part of your routine. The more you practice, the more you will be able to quiet your mind even in the busiest places.

Years earlier, prior to his death, my Uncle Leon said: "When I die, I am going to make it hail on a hot summer's day in July, so you will know that I made it to heaven, and that I am okay." The year I turned fifteen, as I was walking home from the local mall, on a hot summer's day in July, a sudden hail storm hit. I was in shorts, sandals, and a t-shirt, so you can imagine how unprepared I was to run through the marble-sized hail to reach home.

When I burst into the house, I yelled to my mother: "Mom, look outside. Do you know what this means?" She said: "Yes, it means Leon made it to heaven, and he is fine." During that experience, I was able to share with her some messages from Uncle Leon, which only she could recognize and validate as having come from him. After that, she was more open to discussing the limitless possibilities of the world.

Throughout this first experience, I learned that these messages are coming from a place of love, and as the messenger, I need to speak from a place of love as well. I became more diplomatic and asked for permission from the listener, prior to giving messages.

If you are attempting to open a line of communication with someone you love, I can provide one-on-one coaching to assist you in tapping into the Spirit World. As part of my coaching, I can assist you to learn specific techniques that will allow you to find the quiet place in your mind that will allow you to hear what your loved ones are saying, and how to convey their messages to others in a loving way. If you are interested in a coaching session, or attending one of my seminars or workshops, contact me at www.dianewargalla.com.

Chapter 7

Resetting Your GPS: Empowering Your Ability to Choose

When a prediction about the future is received, have you ever wondered where the information is coming from? Where is the future written, and can it be changed?

I was 10 years old, and we had just moved into a new house where, for the first time, I had a bedroom of my own, a backyard, and friends to play with out on the street. My brother, Cliff, was 14 years old, and he was more of everything: taller, more athletic, stronger, and a big prankster. It meant he spent a lot of time teasing me and giving me the kind of grief that only a big brother can give to a little sister.

For example, there was the time we were out with our father in the car, and I heard the radio announcer make reference to a bigamist. I asked what a bigamist was, and Cliff, quickly and with a straight face, answered, "It's a big fog over England." When I asked if that was true, he and our father broke out in laughter and said: "Yes."

It wasn't until years later when I was in high school that the term bigamist came up in a class, and I realized this was not the real meaning of the term. The class broke out laughing when I gave the teacher my definition of the term, and then she gently explained the real definition of the word.

The year I turned 10 was also the year I planted my first garden, at the top of the driveway along the fence that divided our yard and the neighbors. It was just a little garden, 4 by 2 feet, but I was excited to try growing things on my own. My brother decided that he wanted to plant something as well: planting mini-firecrackers placed throughout my garden, all connected with just one fuse. I had never seen firecrackers up close before, so when he invited me to see a surprise in the garden, I was confused by what I was looking at, or the potential outcome. I innocently stood in the driveway, watching as he lit the fuse. That was how I witnessed him blowing up my garden.

His plan went off without a hitch, and he burst into laughter, giving himself praise for a job well done. I was really upset, asking him: "Why did you do that?" Through his laughter, he teased me further by taunting me on how I just stood there and watched it all happen. He thought I would have tried to stop him. The more upset I became, the funnier he seemed to think it was. In search for what I could do or say to make him stop laughing at me, and pay him back for blowing up my garden, I told him: "Oh yeah, well I know how you are going to die!" I repeated my words until I got his attention. When he finally stopped laughing long enough to show the smallest sign of listening, I shared the vision that ran through my mind. It came as if it was in a TV show for personal viewing, and I explained it this way.

We are both grownups leaving one house to go to another, but we are in two separate cars. I don't know why we are in two separate cars, because we are only going a short distance, but we are. Between the house that we are leaving and the house we are driving to, there is a long, straight road that takes up most of the trip. On that road, we come to an intersection where the traffic light has turned red in front of us, and we stop. You are the first car to stop at the white line at the intersection, and I am directly behind you. The sun is going down, and I can see the outline of your head and shoulders through your back window, and I know it's you. When the light turns green, you quickly hit the gas, and your car jumps into the intersection. Just as you enter the intersection, out of nowhere, a speeding truck running the red light hits your car in the driver's door, pushing you sideways through the intersection, and I see you die.

After sharing this story with him, Cliff became very quiet and walked away. As children, we continued to laugh, love, and drive each other crazy, as most siblings do, and never spoke of it again.

Years later, I was married and moving from one home to another. This was back in the days before cell phones. We had friends and family helping us, as well as individuals who were dropping by to see if they could help us with the move. Since it was Friday, a work day, volunteers came and went throughout the day. As we were packing the moving truck, certain items were deemed to be too fragile or important to be stored in the truck for the trip to the new house. So, those items were put aside in a pile by the front door for me to load into my car and take to our new home.

However, in the midst of this packing, I had to leave and pick up the keys to the new house from the lawyer, and when I returned, everyone had left with the truck and were on their way to the new house. I started loading up the fragile items that were left behind, when my brother, with his great timing, showed up and gave me a helping hand. It was just the two of us, alone at my old house. It was fun to chat with him as we evaluated what still needed to be packed.

We pressed his car into service and loaded it up with those items that wouldn't fit in mine—delicate items, such as lamps, pictures, and plants—and then locked up the house and started our journey to my new home.

It was coming on to dusk and, in typical big brother fashion, Cliff offered to lead the way. I said it was not a problem, and off we went. We were moving from northern Mississauga to the south end. As part of the trip, we headed down a long, straight stretch of road, called Winston Churchill Boulevard. The road wasn't busy, and as it was later in the day, I hadn't flipped my lights on yet, but the lengthening shadows meant it was only a matter of time before I did.

We pulled up to a traffic light at one of the highway intersections and stopped. While I was thinking about what to pick up for dinner and how many people we needed to feed, my brother was having separate thoughts of his own, consisting of déjà vu. His déjà vu went from fuzziness to clarity when it suddenly occurred to him that the surroundings matched the story I had told him all those years ago, when he was 14 years old. The whole story, when we were children, flooded his mind, and as it did, he put the car in park and turned on his four-way flashers. I was directly behind him, wondering what was wrong, and thought he might be having car problems. When the light turned green, Cliff left his car in the parked position and stayed seated. Within a split second of the light turning green, a big, heavy truck entered the intersection from the highway just beyond our view, ran the red light, and barreled through the intersection. Startled by the sudden appearance of the truck, it occurred to me that someday that driver was going to cause an accident.

With his flashers still on, I rolled down my window and pulled up beside his car to ask what was wrong. Cliff waved me on, and I could see his mouth saying: "Go, go...." He didn't appear to be in any trouble, so I continued through the intersection and pulled off to the side of the road further ahead. Watching him through my side and rear-view mirror, I wondered if I should turn around and go back to him, but he didn't get out of his car to lift his hood, so I just waited. During one of the red lights, he finally turned off his flashers, and then, on the next green light, he pulled forward and stopped behind me on the side of the road. I went to get out of my car, to find out what had happened, but he just yelled out his window for me to keep going and that he would follow me. He seemed pretty adamant about it—like he wasn't just calmly saying it—he was ordering me. Despite my curiosity, I knew the only way I was going to find out what happened was to get to the new house.

I got back in my car and continued on to our new home, which was in a crescent cul-de-sac. It had two entrances off of a main road. I went in the first entrance to my street, and Cliff drove forward and went in through the second one. When we got to my house, we were facing each other on opposite sides of the road. As he got out of the car, it was clear that he was distraught. As we walked toward each other, he started yelling at me, "You f***ing witch!!"

I tried to ask him what was wrong, but he kept yelling at me. Then, Cliff started repeating back to me the story I had told him so long ago. Everything fell into place for me as he talked, and it occurred to me that was the truck, and he should have died, but he didn't. My vision had played out differently than the reality we had just experienced. The whole sequence came into stark clarity. I had given my brother the information, but he had the free will to change that story—to change his destiny.

For a second, I thanked my 10-year-old self for being annoyed enough to share that information. My intention back then might not have been the best, but this was the best outcome I could have hoped for.

Resetting Your GPS: Empowering Your Ability to Choose

When we physically came together, standing in the middle of the street, the two of us embraced and held each other. We were both shaking with amazement, as well as disbelief about how differently that could have gone. Questions of *"how did you know?"* bounced back and forth between us. I was grateful that he had remembered it at all. We were both very grateful that he was able to change the outcome, just by being aware of the story. He had the ability to create a different ending, one that changed how and when he died, making it into a future event once more.

In many respects, when I give information like this to individuals, I am really giving them the ability to choose a different path or to make alternative choices in their life's journey. I am not deciding the course of their journey but giving them a better understanding of the possibilities in front of them. I am seeing a trajectory of what someone's future can look like at that moment. But there are so many factors that can alter our trajectory. All I can do is share the information, giving them the ability to make decisions, with the best information possible.

My mother also had a similar experience with her own brother. She received an intuitive message that her brother, Leon, was going to die on his wedding day, and without giving him any prior warning, he did. I saw this high probability vision of how my brother would pass, but he didn't. Your free will allows you to make choices and decide for yourself how you will act and react. My vision, and my mother's vision, didn't negate our brothers' free will. Would Uncle Leon have had a different outcome if my mother had shared what she knew? Would that have impacted the choices he made that night? We won't know, but perhaps that was her way of allowing him to express his free will, without the burden of her vision.

It wasn't that my mother or I had any control over any of this. It was their free will that made it happen or didn't make it happen. Seeing the future and a possibility of something happening in a circumstance of nature, or in the life of another, even their possible passing, does not mean that the holder of that knowledge has the responsibility to change that destiny. That is their personal journey. Sharing the information with them relieves the holder of that knowledge, while empowering the recipient with additional knowledge, options, and tools to better equip them in their decision-making process.

I might give them the information straight up or use a story to tell them what I received, or it could be a simple reminder of something that they might want to consider, like wearing their seatbelt consistently. I find that whenever I intuitively receive information about a person's future, whether it is prosperous or challenging, the sharing of that information can be a special challenge of its own.

When the information is positive, it's obviously easy to share, but when it is challenging news, the person may simply not be in a place to receive it, although I strive to provide an empowering resolution to that challenge. The resolution is offered as an alternative direction that person can take to help them through or completely avoid that challenging situation. There is no need or necessity for me to give anyone any challenging information about their future, if I ever thought for a second that they were not in control and did not have free will to change the outcome.

Whatever the circumstances that I happen to know, I have learned that there is a reason that I have this information. It helps to prepare me to be there for them, come what may. It allows me to clear my schedule and be there for someone so that they are not alone during that time, especially when it is challenging circumstances that I see in my vision. They receive the love and support that they need from me and those around them. I have found it to be beneficial to my life to have that insider connection to this key information, in order to help people. When I share this information with individuals, I also search through the cosmos for the information to help them to find the best possible way to navigate those challenging circumstances, so they make the best possible choices.

Preparing myself for a challenge, such as a death, is more difficult when the message I receive is in direct relation to the people I love. Yes, even I find it difficult to see loved ones leave. One of these instances happened when my partner, Jack, told me he had followed through with my son's request about getting a new suit, and texted the name, location, and available date of a tailor who comes to Canada quarterly. Conveniently, the tailor would be working out of my son, Scott's, hometown within the next few weeks. It was a one-day-only event, where the tailor was making appointments, working out of a hotel room to receive clients and take measurements, and orders, on custom-made shirts and suits.

Resetting Your GPS: Empowering Your Ability to Choose

Now, that information on its own sounds like good news for everyone, except for the fact that when Jack shared that information with me, the voice within my mind said, "Oh, good; Scott will have the suit back in time for the funeral." I was shocked to receive this message because there were no sick relatives or pending demises, so my analytical mind responded with the inner question: "What? Whose funeral?" To which I received the answer: "Brother."

I then asked Jack how long it takes for a suit to be ready once the order is placed. He told me the turnaround time is very fast. It could easily be ready in 2–3 weeks.

Knowing this upcoming funeral was in relation to a brother energy, it could literally mean the passing of my other son, William, or my brother, Cliff. I immediately shared this information with Jack. Not wanting to know anything more about it, I stopped asking questions and, in my mind's eye, put a protective energy bubble of health and safety around both my sons and my brother, which became my primary focus in the weeks to come.

In the past, when I've received similar messages, I have learned that if I ask for more detail with clarifying questions (such as, "Is it the brother energy coming from my parallel generation, the generation above, or below?"), in my mind's voice, I receive the answers. Once I've established the generation the brother energy is coming from, I narrow it down to see if it is an actual brother, brother-in-law, cousin, or someone who is like a brother. Then, by process of elimination based on the answers I receive, I narrow down whose brotherly energy it is and who is scheduled to pass.

I then go on to ask how they will pass, followed by when, to learn when it will take place in relation to other scheduled activities or the time of year. In this instance, I already knew it was in relation to the tailor and his ability to produce a suit.

Had this been a message of another family tree and not mine, I would have dug deeper for more details. But I knew, no matter who it was, that I, and all the people I care about and love, would be deeply affected by the loss, and I became instantly fearful that it was my son.

As it turned out, the appointment date with the tailor clashed with the exact same date as my granddaughter's birthday party. During the festivities, I asked my son, Scott, how he made out with his appointment that morning ordering a suit.

He said the timing and preparation for the birthday party made it difficult for him to honor the appointment, and he had to cancel. On the outside, I simply responded: "Oh, that's too bad; I understand." But on the inside, I was doing the happy dance and, with my inner voice, asked the Spirit World, since there isn't going to be a suit made, does that mean there isn't going to be a funeral? In the absence of a reply, I built up the courage to check in with my brother, Cliff's, energy, and when I concluded he was fine and safe, I continued to build and hold a protective bubble around my sons.

Eight days later, on a Sunday afternoon, while walking through the doors of the local Canadian Tire store, my phone rang, and I saw it was Scott calling. I couldn't hear him very well at first and had to step outside to get a better signal. When I did, I clearly heard him say: "Mom, I have bad news."

There it was: the call! Overwhelmed with anticipation, my body weakened, and my throat closed as I choked out the words: "What's wrong?"

He responded: "Uncle Rick is in the hospital, and it doesn't look good."

Shocked by his answer, I struggled to process the shifting of my thoughts from my son, William, to my brother-in-law, Rick, and it left me speechless. When he finished telling me what had happened, there was a pregnant pause of silence from my side of the phone. Breaking the silence, he asked: "Are you okay?" Now, with tears flowing, I could barely get the words out: "I thought it was your brother."

He jumped in and responded with: "No, no; Willam's okay. He's with me. I had a job to do this weekend, and he gave me a hand. We've been together all day." Putting his cell on speaker phone, I heard him say: "Hey, William; say hi to Mom." I sobbed with relief when I heard William say: "Hi Mom; what's up?"

They shared how their father's brother, their Uncle Rick, was in the intensive care unit of North York General Hospital, after returning from vacation in the

Resetting Your GPS: Empowering Your Ability to Choose

Dominican Republic. Two days before his return, he had become ill with what was at first thought to be Montezuma's revenge. Within days of being home, his symptoms of fever, diarrhea, and dehydration continued, which led to a variety of complications, including an extremely low white blood cell count, septic shock, and kidney failure.

The last time I saw Rick was two years earlier, when we met by chance in the small village in which I live. We shared a summer's drink, a hug, and I told him I loved him.

When Rick and I were in our early twenties, he discovered my gift of knowing when someone was going to die or be in an accident. He made me promise that if I ever picked up anything about him, I would tell him.

The day after I received Scott's call, I packed a bag and headed to Toronto to see Rick. Upon my arrival on his ward, I was instructed on how to properly put on a sterilized gown, gloves, and face mask by hospital staff. Then I was led into his room, where I was greeted by his loving confidant, Lisa, who was protectively watching over him.

Lisa welcomed me with open arms and informed Rick of my arrival. With his eyes now open, unable to speak due to the medical apparatus invading his vocal cords, Rick was able to communicate through slight movement of his head and toes, and by moving his finger, and an occasional squeeze of his hand as he dozed in and out of consciousness. Upon saying hello to Lisa, I approached Rick's bedside, extending my arm, intending to put my hand in his to say hello. It was a wonderful feeling when I noticed he had lifted his finger to greet me.

Lisa and I stayed on either side of the bed, doing our best to keep up his spirits with small talk about anything we could think of that was unrelated to the issues within the room, and even included the occasional rhetorical question directed to him for good measure.

Although we had noble intentions and made a valiant effort, it wasn't long before we heart wrenchingly found ourselves standing quietly at Rick's bedside, watching over him as he drifted in and out of consciousness.

Without uttering a word of why I had arrived, or my intention of what I wanted to do for him, I brought my attention back into the moment and started giving Rick Therapeutic Touch (TT). TT is a natural healing modality that I learned years ago, which is similar to the healing techniques of Native Shamanic Healers and is known throughout the world for its ability to boost the immune system and assist the body to heal. Quietly, Lisa watched the relaxed movement of my hands sweeping above the surface of Rick's body from top to bottom. We both giggled when she was compelled to tell him that I was giving him my *voodoo* to help him get better.

Once finished, and with Rick resting quietly, she and I sat off to the side of the room and quietly spoke of his condition. She enlightened me on how a normal white blood cell count, the blood cells that keep us healthy by fighting germs, can range anywhere from 4.5 to 11 in a healthy person. Unbeknown to them as to why, Rick's white blood cell count was currently sitting at 1. With no immune system to speak of, our gowns that we were asked to wear were not to protect us from him, but rather meant to protect him from further germ exposure from us. Based on the process of elimination of the blood work and variety of tests being performed, the negative results continued to puzzle his doctors, who continued the cocktail of all known antibiotics in hopes that it might make a difference.

Later that afternoon, as evening approached, Lisa had to leave. While in the process of putting her belongings together, she mentioned Rick's sister, Lauri, was on her way, and I offered to stay with Rick until she arrived. Now alone in the room with Rick, who was sleeping in a semi-conscious state, he and I were able to speak freely through mental telepathy. The experience of hearing his strong, healthy voice speaking in my mind's ear was a complete contradiction to the same man in my eyes' view, who was unable to speak at all, and who was fighting for his life.

I shared the story of Scott and the tailor, and I told him I neglected to follow up in order to find out who the message was in reference to. I would never know if things could have been different, but what I did say now was that I was sorry! I was sorry I didn't have the guts to figure it out and come to him earlier. Rick, on the other hand, brushed off my concerns as a non-issue, and brought his deceased father forward into the conversation. Now hearing both their voices, and his father Ron's distinctive laughter, they let me know they were together and in good hands.

For the days to follow, I continued sending Therapeutic Touch remotely, and received daily updates about his condition through his sister, Lauri, as an extension of his daughter, Kimber-lee's, updates.

Two weeks and one day following the date of the tailor coming to town, I received a call letting me know that my brother-in-law, Rick, at age 63, had just moments earlier passed, with the cause of death undetermined. Within hours of receiving that call, I received notification that my Uncle Elize, my father's brother, had gone to bed the night before and transitioned back to spirit the very same day, peacefully in his sleep. Although neither of these amazing men were in my day-to-day life, I loved them very much, and knowing they are no longer walking among us makes the world feel just a little emptier.

Because the mind does not distinguish between real or imaginary fear, taking action when consumed with any type of fear takes courage.

Upon receiving the message of a pending funeral in regard to a brother energy within the next few weeks, I decided to take a clear course of action to embrace my fear and change its form from a potential disabling position, into empowerment, by focusing on nothing else other than my sons' protection and health. The skill to move forward in the presence of fear does not come easily, but it can be taught, learned, and mastered over time.

You, too, have the capability of changing your fear energy and transforming it into protective energy for your loved ones, as well as yourself, with an exercise I like to call *The Bubble*. Years ago, I heard a mother make reference to her children, stating: "I can't put a bubble around them, you know. I just have to let them get hurt and learn." Which led me to the question: "Why can't I put a protective bubble around them? That would work!"

You can start the exercise by seeing the person, people, or object, such as a car or a home that you want to put a protective bubble around, clearly in your mind's eye. If need be, you can use the aid of a photograph of that person, people, or object, to help imprint the image in your mind.

Using the creativity of your imagination, see the image clearly in your mind's eye as though it were alive and right in front of you. As an example of what I do to bring the image alive, when it is a person, a family, or a group of people I wish to protect, I imagine them smiling and waving to me, and I smile and wave back. This brings my awareness directly to them, and theirs to me.

Now that the recipient of your protective intention is clearly in your mind's eye, you can now place them in the center of a protective bubble of your choice. What your bubble looks like is entirely up to you. I personally like to change it up and allow my imagination to flow. Sometimes the bubble looks exactly like a thin, clear luminous bubble, much like the watery soap bubbles children play with. The only difference between a child's soap bubble and mine, is that I place the intention that my bubble cannot be popped or penetrated. Only love, health, and protection can flow through the bubble and reach them. Everything else bounces off. Another one of my favorite images is to put a series of randomly placed, electrically charged circles of thread that spin around the image I wish to protect. This too is indestructible, and only love, health, and protection can enter its walls and make it stronger.

I regularly place a bubble around myself, and a separate bubble for the vehicles in which I, and any of my passengers, ride in. I have also been known to place a protective bubble around a country, a leader, and even the world.

What will your protective bubble look like, and where will you place it?

Chapter 8

Clyde's Story: What a High Vibrational Life Looks Like

In my cravings for a spiritual mentor and a partner, I decided to join a dating website to get out and socialize. I was confident that the universe was going to give me the partner I craved. This person was going to be a truly remarkable individual, a superior communicator who understood that we are spirits having a human experience. He would have a similar mindset as myself, dedicating himself to live a high vibrational lifestyle. So, I put a keyword into my description of all the things I like to do, along with the word, *aura*.

When a potential suitor asked me what an aura was, I explained an aura is a living vibration that appears as a subtle, illuminated quality, or atmosphere, seen as emanating from a person, place, or thing. If they seemed disinterested or uninformed on the general topic concerning a higher self, or a much larger living environment beyond the physical, I would thank them for their time, wish them well in their search, and then continue my search for a partner. I knew they were not who I was looking for.

I do not believe in coincidence. When two or more similar or related events occur at the same time, without any planning, I recognize these moments as the universe speaking to me as a form of communication, and I take notice. Part of my criteria I asked the universe for was that when I met the person I was meant to be with, I would receive concrete proof that this person was the right individual for me.

When I first heard from Clyde, he immediately mentioned the word aura, as seen on my profile, telling me that he was fascinated with them, and that he had several books on the topic of energy fields, as well as books on consciousness and other states of reality. I was immediately intrigued.

We spoke briefly through instant messages and over the phone; then, he insisted we meet face-to-face, to see if there was chemistry between us. When we met in person, what was meant to be a quick get-together for coffee, turned into eight hours of friendly banter, and catching up on the first fifty years of our lives. Driving in separate cars, we continued our chat at a nearby restaurant, in which Clyde ordered and picked up the tab for our lobster bisque lunch, and I remember thinking to myself: "This guy must really like me!" He had the most beaming smile and was a master of the English language, down to the smallest detail. I loved his expressive personality. Using descriptive phrases, he created amazing pictures of his enthralling life and adventures, which filled my head, and made me laugh and feel as though I were actually there.

Our conversation wandered to the pictures he had posted on his profile. What caught my eye were his descriptions of the people in the photos, how they met, the purpose of each event, and his sharing what they all meant to him.

Leading the Dragon Boat parade, Clyde Boom to the far right, Lucy to the left of the float, and me to the far left.

Clyde's Story: What a High Vibrational Life Looks Like

The first was an action shot of *Kindred Spirits,* which was the name of his fun-filled dragon boat team. The picture showed an annual event on Toronto Island, with the team marching in a parade they created, before each race, while on route to the starting line. They had a 3-D, man-made, wooden replica of a dragon. It was approximately eight-feet long with a ten-foot wingspan, and there were soap bubbles that danced in the air from the dragon's behind, leaving a trail behind its path. All the team members, family, and friends were dancing along to an uplifting array of party tunes that were playing from inside the beast's belly, giving the distinct message that the party had arrived.

The second shot was a Christmas parade float with an assortment of life-size Nutcrackers, each carrying an instrument, such as a horn, drum, or trombone. It also was accompanied by the music of a fully instrumental marching band, to which he had personally contributed the sound track, just as he had for the dragon boat team. I heard how the Santa Claus parade was hosted each year by the Bolton Kinsmen, which he was a member of, and how each member participated by building their own Nutcracker creations with recycled materials. His Nutcracker included a large plastic bucket for a drum, in his favorite color, blue.

The next was a picture that he referred to as *his gal.* It was a photo of his dog, Lucy, dressed in a hat and scarf, wearing her favorite sunglasses. These were followed by two independent shots of Clyde. Someone had captured a classic moment of Clyde talking, hand gestures and all, during his fiftieth birthday party. He was dressed in an Elvis Presley outfit, with sequins all over it, that he and his friend, Susan, had spent joyous hours putting together. The last image portrayed a calm and relaxed Clyde, sitting outside on a bale of hay by a blazing fire, during a New Year's Eve party, with the silhouette of his friends in the background.

Clyde was very active in his community, and our conversation included the story of a fundraising hockey event the Bolton Kinsmen had planned to host on a natural pond. But just prior to the event, the pond began to thaw, making it bumpy, uneven, and unusable. Then, he recalled how it was lucky that his friend, Cary, who was a fireman, was able to help them out by reflooding the pond, which then froze again overnight, making it smooth, firm, and ready for the event.

I couldn't help but wonder if this might be the same Cary I had grown up with. After all, how many guys named Cary, who became a fireman, could there possibly be? Cary was an adventurous guy who loved nature. If you wanted to have an adventure in nature with someone who was an expert in survival skills, then he was the person you would want by your side. We would seek each other out at school reunions and catch up on what was new in our lives, including the fact that he had become a fireman. He was near and dear to my heart.

Clyde's description of Cary seemed very familiar, so I asked what his buddy's last name was. He told me, and I responded with: "Does he still have a mustache?" That's when we realized that we both knew the same man. I was able to rekindle my friendship with Cary, and it was just another example of how well Clyde and I fit together.

I saw this as a sign from the universe: the one I had asked for to confirm this was the right person for me. He was the guy that I was supposed to be with. I was okay with that. Our relationship blossomed quickly because we fascinated each other.

As Clyde and I went through the next year together, we shared moments just like these described in the photos, and many more. I joined him and his friends, passing out Mars bars to the spectators at the Santa Clause parade, becoming a cheerleader at all his Dragon Boat races, and dancing to the tunes that bellowed out of the dragon float's belly, inviting all the spectators to join in. They made me one of their own, without hesitation.

In his profile, one of the words that captured my attention above all others was the phrase, *New Age*. I was intrigued, and he knew it. He was the son of a Baptist minister and a highly religious mother. Clyde also had a photographic memory, which made him a living library of everything he had ever experienced, heard, or read. Although he proclaimed to be nonreligious due to his upbringing, he could quote the Bible verbatim, unlike anyone I had ever met. As a young man determined to find the answers to his questions about the origins of the world and its history, Clyde studied and became proficient in the practice of all major religions around the globe.

Clyde's Story: What a High Vibrational Life Looks Like

In spite of his choice not to practice any particular religion, on his own terms, Clyde had a very fulfilling relationship with his creator, in which he gave thanks for his blessings every evening as he expressed them out loud prior to turning in for the night. I remember one afternoon when Clyde received a tweet from one of his over 20,000 followers on Twitter. This woman had misquoted a passage of the Bible for her own personal recognition, with a personal jab to discredit him. Livid by her misquote of the Biblical passage for personal gain and an attempt to shame him, Clyde jumped out of his seat to a standing position, yelling at his computer as though she could hear him. Now reseated, leaning back in his chair, he grabbed his keyboard and corrected not only her quote but the spelling errors that he found in her original tweet.

Clyde was committed to self-improvement and was riveted by the supernatural. He desired to find the answers to the questions of our creation, Atlantis, reincarnation, telepathy, meditation, yoga, parallel universes, quantum physics, mediumship, power of intention, auras, tarot cards, crystal healing, ghosts, quantum jumping, remote viewing, extrasensory perception (ESP), and so much more. You name it, if it was unexplainable, a natural health alternative or a conspiracy theory, you can bet he was studying and researching it. I had never met anyone with so much enthusiasm to unlock life's mysteries, and with so much in common with me, in my whole life.

He was up-to-date and well-versed on these and many other topics and was open to discussion at any time. Other than a distinct memory of a previous life that he lived during the time of Atlantis, which he was able to describe down to the smallest detail of its existence, and his desire to stop reincarnating, Clyde claimed to have very little self-awareness beyond his five senses. His fascination was based more on interest than personal experience. My instincts told me otherwise. I had chosen to discover my gifts organically through personal experience. Imagine the two of us discussing these topics: me with my personal experience, as I learned organically all about them; and Clyde with his wealth of knowledge through books, seminars, and workshops, with all this knowledge and curiosity openly shared through his photographic mind.

He quickly introduced me to his favorite authors, such as Tony Robbins, Deepak Chopra, Wayne Dyer, David Icke, and more. Our combined energy lit up a room. We were magic and started working together right away. As adults, we were building a relationship. One day, the invitation came to spend the night. It was then that I had to tell him about the nightmares that I was having as a lingering effect of the post-traumatic stress disorder (PTSD), following a car accident I was involved in a few years earlier.

Then, he said: "Oh, that's easy. Come here." We sat down with pen and paper. He then showed me how to write an affirmation with the intention of resetting my sleeping pattern. He reminded me that I have the power to create my own reality based on what I believe, what I think to be true, how I speak, and what I focus on, which included my sleeping hours. I needed that reminder in the face of what I was dealing with. It was about creating a vision, and focusing on that vision as being already true, then being open to the universe bringing it into reality, just as the universe brought him to me.

I would stand in front of the mirror, and look into the reflection of my own eyes, while saying this affirmation: "I am going to have a restful and peaceful sleep. Knowing I am the creator of my dreams, I am going to have relaxing, calm, and inspiring dreams. I am going to wake peacefully in the morning, remembering my dreams, and they are going to be wonderful."

I taped the affirmation on my bathroom mirror, and then Clyde made a copy and taped it to the bathroom mirror that I used at his home as well. I would recite this to myself, each night, with complete confidence that the intention of my words would guide my subconscious thoughts and direct my sleep accordingly. Then, I would give myself a big smile and blow myself a kiss. It worked! The nightmares instantly began to ease. I had two nightmares that first week and noticed that when my dreams started heading off track the least little bit, going down a dark or negative path, I would redirect them, because I had control over my dreams.

Little by little, our romantic relationship grew. It was the most amazing relationship that I could have found. We shared our lives and knowledge. He was naturally happy and we understood each other. I felt as though I belonged and had found my people.

Our desks were placed back to back at opposite ends in his home office, with a large, open space between us. When I cleaned out the desk that was designed to be mine, he gave me a box to put all the files into it that were in the desk drawers. As I was taking them out of the desk and putting them in the box, one page seemed to leap out of the files and landed on the floor, face up, at my feet.

When I picked it up, the content caught my attention. Not only was each sentence one to five words in length, and centered on the page, but they started out with the words: "She's blonde." Each sentence was another block in a description of a woman that sounded a lot like me. Things, such as New Age, loves dogs, infectious laugh, and entrepreneurial mindset, were written on this page. It was such an easy read. I didn't mean to pry, but it jumped out at me, and there it was.

I turned to Clyde and asked him what it was. When he saw what I had in my hand, he smiled, and then leaned way back in his chair and crossed his arms. Then he told me to read it to him. So, I did.

"Who is that?" he asked me.

"Well, it's me. When did you write it?"

"Two years ago. What took you so long to come into my life?"

I laughed, and said, "I'm sorry. I was busy getting a divorce."

"Good answer. Don't take so long next time," he said.

Clyde had a belief in the power of manifesting reality, a belief I discovered and shared with him. He became my business mentor and spiritual supporter. Our businesses were intertwined as we relied on each other's strengths to accomplish our goals and spark creativity. We would remind each other to take breaks away from the office. We would take long walks with his dog, Lucy, through the Albion Hills Conservation Area, and when weather permitted, have a picnic lunch by the river, and work long into the night.

He had a passion for music, with a personal collection that would match any professional collector. True to form, he had memorized the composer's names, musicians, and lyrics for each song in his entire collection. As part of his bucket list, Clyde wanted to be a musician and sing in front of a live audience. He studied music and the guitar. He wrote lyrics for his personal use, and even went so far as to purchase a professional drum set, two full-size organs, and several electric guitars, along with microphones and speakers. He had everything for a band to come together, and he had it all in his basement in a soundproof room. Music was such a part of our daily life, and we loved it.

The first time he heard me sing, he stood up and clapped as if he was attending some great concert and I was the main attraction. After that, he would deliberately play the songs he knew I enjoyed singing, and he was my captive audience. We joined a choir, where we sang the part of two turtle doves in a Christmas recital. Everything we did was so much fun.

Clyde as lead singer.

Clyde inspired me to write a book to share my personal experiences so that the average person could understand what is possible for them as well. He encouraged me to participate in his vision board, making it ours. It was an 8' x 8' cork board, strategically placed on the wall so it would be the first thing we saw in the morning and the last thing we saw at the end of our work day. Shortly after we met, he had taken down everything that was on the board, so that we could start fresh on a joint vision. It truly became our board. We started out putting all the things that represented our dreams for immediate manifestations and goals for the future. One of his goals was to increase his

Clyde's Story: What a High Vibrational Life Looks Like

Twitter followers. He would print off his statistics showing his current followers, then put up each of his goals for the number of followers he wanted. It started off with just a 1,000, but as he met each goal, he added another one. He ended up with over 20,000 followers on Twitter.

He was not a celebrity of any sort, or politician in the public eye. He was simply an extraordinary man who generously solved other people's problems when it came to understanding computer programs. He built a large following by genuinely giving of himself. He was listed as Ontario's largest Twitter leader, which was quite a feat at that time for a computer author.

On the vision board, we also had my book cover. I had begun writing this book actually. I added my dream home, with water in front of it. He put up a picture of the sound room for his music, and a spiral staircase he wanted, with a secondary walk-out from the basement. We had a riding lawn mower, an all-terrain-vehicle, fishing boats and canoes, and so much more. It was very detailed to say the least.

The board grew as we went along, including the addition of happy faces. Clyde had always wanted to be in a rock n' roll band and sing as the lead singer in front of a live audience. To my surprise, that Christmas, it manifested into reality. We had gone with friends to a Bolton Kinsmen party, which we were members of, for a formal Christmas dinner. After dinner, there was going to be a band playing in the basement, and they were setting up their equipment on the stage. Just as dinner was wrapping up, Clyde told me he was going to go check out the band and would be right back. A few moments later, I heard one of our friends yelling up the stairwell, "Diane, come quick! Clyde's singing!" I ran downstairs to find him on stage with the band. Within minutes of him meeting them, they had made a connection. For that entire night, he was the band's lead singer. He sang in front of the restaurant's clients, staff, and more than thirty of his closest friends, who had stayed to enjoy the music.

Throughout the evening, several of us would be his backup singers, providing the doo-wop and harmony. We had so much fun, and it was a blast! Clyde was busy working out the songs they would sing after the break, and the manager of the restaurant took me aside to tell me this was the first night trying out this new band. He asked if Clyde and I were professionals and if we would be interested in coming back another night. I laughed hysterically and said: "No, we're not professionals. I'll let Clyde know of your offer, but this may be a one-time event. We're just having fun!" He gave me his business card.

As we started the new year, Clyde got all his business administration up to date. He had a desire to start cleaning house and get his affairs in order for the year ahead. He kept saying: "I need to wrap this up." But that wasn't all he took care of. He made an appointment with the lawyer to have his will updated, as it hadn't been changed since he had become a widower, ten years earlier. He also made an appointment for his annual medical checkup.

Clyde was the author of several educational books on the topic of Linux. He published both the teachers' and students' versions and sold them to colleges and universities. This year, his focus was on Twitter: how to reach the masses and use Twitter as a business tool. He seemed inspired and determined to get everything in order, and that is what he did.

One Friday afternoon, I walked into Clyde's with my overnight bag for the weekend. As I walked into the room where the vision board was kept, I was shocked to see that a year's worth of dreams, accomplishments, and future plans were completely gone! Shaken by the vast emptiness of the wall, my bag slipped out of my fingers and dropped to the floor with a thud. As I stared at the empty wall, not knowing what this meant, I felt the blood drain from my face, and the churning of my stomach preparing itself to vomit.

Clyde ran up behind me, taking my hand to turn me around to see his face, and said: "It's okay! I had an epiphany."

Then he explained that he woke up that morning and realized that there were things that were not going to happen anymore. So, he started removing those things off our vision board, and before he knew it, the board was empty. Still confused, I asked: "None of it is going to happen?" He went on to share that there were a few things that he felt were still going to come into reality, and he had placed them in a pile, on the TV stand in the corner of the room, as he had not put them back on the board yet. Then he told me that there was going to be something even bigger happening. When I asked to see what he had put aside—what was still going to happen—he said there was time for that later. Clyde said we weren't going to work this weekend; he wanted to spend time together doing whatever we wanted to do and enjoy ourselves.

Clyde's Story: What a High Vibrational Life Looks Like

Clyde had acquired a library of books that filled an entire wall, with information about spirituality, new scientific discoveries, and topics of interest that we would take turns reading to each other on a daily basis. That weekend, we took Lucy for long walks, visited friends, laid on the pull-out couch in his office while watching David Icke documentaries, ate our favorite foods, and read to each other.

After putting the chesterfield back together and putting the coffee table back in place, Clyde shared that he had a signed organ donor card, and he wanted to know, in my gut, how I felt about him being an organ donor. My first response was to tell him that if that was what he wanted to do, then he should do it. "That's your head talking. What's in your heart; what's your instinct telling you?" he asked.

So, I told him that I was getting the feeling that they would take his body away from me, and that I would never see him again. "Okay," he said. Then he took the card out of his wallet, tore it in half, and set it on the coffee table. Surprised by his actions, I told him that organ donation was a good thing, and if he wanted to donate, he should. He said, not if my instincts were telling me different, and he didn't want that to happen to me. It was clear he trusted my instincts.

Now, I could not help but mention that he was just fifty-one years old. This was a man who took care of himself. He jogged or walked every day, took vitamins, ate live organic foods, and drank high vibrational fluoride and chemical free water, out of a glass water dispenser in his kitchen. I asked if there was something he needed to tell me. He laughed and said he was fine—that he felt an amazing clarity and excitement that something phenomenal was about to happen—and he was planning on sharing it with me and living to the age of ninety. He simply wanted to cover this with me. I chalked it up to the cleaning house mood that he had been in since the new year.

Our bucket lists came up next, and he shared that singing with the band at Christmas had been on the list. Then he shared that he felt blessed; his list was pretty full, and he had done almost everything on it, including meeting and falling in love with me. When I asked him about the vision board, he said that my book was going to be written, and he described what my career would look like after it was done, in terms of teaching, speaking, and inspiring others on a vast scale. He did not want to talk about his part of the vision board but kept saying how motivated it made him feel, and with each passing day, he could tell it was drawing closer. Although he could not put his finger on it or describe what it looked like, he said he could feel a new beginning was about to take place, and he was excited right down to his core to discover what it was, and for it to reveal itself.

I left Monday morning and went back home to do some personal errands, and he invited me back for that night. When I returned, he told me he had a headache, which was unusual for him. In fact, he was resting when I arrived. We went to bed at midnight, after having a fabulous evening together. It had been filled with laughter, silliness, and teasing, and once we kissed goodnight, I turned and put my back up next to him. Within seconds, I felt him moving. At first, I thought he was continuing our silliness, but when I rolled over, expecting to continue our horsing around, I realized that he was in trouble and having a seizure.

I bolted out of bed and ran around to his side to grab the phone to call 911. I answered all their questions and followed the instructions to roll him over on his left side until paramedics arrived, as they were on their way. I was told she could not hold on the line, and to call back if it got worse. The seizure continued, and I used pillows up against his back to keep him propped up on his side.

Feeling completely helpless, I continued telling him that help was on its way and that he was going to be fine. In those long, long moments before help arrived, I searched my thoughts for what I could do next to help him. I knew I had to run down to unlock the front door for the paramedics to come in. Lucy, who slept at the foot of the bed, had to be put in the backyard, because I knew she would not let anyone get near him, and I did not want her to interfere with the paramedics.

Once they arrived, the paramedics hooked him up to machines and started monitoring his vital signs. They said he was going to have to go to the hospital. I asked if it would be possible for me to ride in the ambulance with him. At first, they said yes, but then they changed their minds and asked me to find another way to the hospital. That was fine with me, because Clyde was the focus.

Clyde's Story: What a High Vibrational Life Looks Like

They were in communication with the hospital and sat in front of the house for quite a while. I could see their silhouettes through the back window of the ambulance, and I knew it was bad. Clyde's close friend, Cary, was a fire Chief in Toronto, and lived just a short drive up the highway. Knowing him as I did, I knew that he would be very supportive during this emergency. I did not want to be alone, so I phoned his home. His wife, Cathy, answered and said he was working, but within moments, she appeared in the driveway and drove with me to the hospital.

When we arrived at the hospital and asked how he was, they put Cathy and me in a private room. I looked at her and said: "This isn't a good sign, to put us in a private room. Something is really wrong." I tried my hardest to connect in with him through the Spirit World, but it was fuzzy, and I could not make a solid connection with him. Normally, when I connect in with the Spirit World, I can tell if someone is currently residing in a body or not. But if people have Alzheimer's, are experiencing post-traumatic stress disorder, or they are in a coma—what I would call the in-between states, from the Spirit World to the natural world—they can come through as though they do not have a body. That was how Clyde was coming through to me, but they had not said he had passed. They just said that they were working on him.

We waited in the private room for what felt like an eternity, and then a surgeon came in. He told me how sorry he was, but even if Clyde had been right in front of them at the hospital, there was nothing that they could have done for him. He had a brain aneurysm at the base of his skull, at the spinal column, and it had ruptured. The most beautiful mind in the world was now non-functioning. But his heart had not caught onto that idea yet. He was still alive physically, but he was not coming back. No words can express how devastated I felt as those words sunk in.

I had brought Clyde's phone with us, but I had never used his phone before. Somehow, I managed to figure it out. Between Cathy and me, we started making phone calls to his closest family and friends, spreading the word that he was in the hospital and he was not coming back, and if they wanted to see him alive one more time, then they needed to come here right away and say their goodbyes. Everyone, who we called, dropped what was going on in their lives, and they came, one by one, marching in that door.

Once they had told me of his condition, the hospital staff brought me to where he was in the ICU. I could see all the machines that he was hooked up to, which were helping to keep him alive.

Clyde and I, in all of our discussions, had discussed our belief in a living spirit that superseded a physical living body, which meant that even if a person was considered to have no brain activity whatsoever, they would still know what was going on around them. I do not believe in coincidence at all, and here he was, in the situation that we had discussed. So, I pulled a chair up to the top of the bed, where I could lean forward and be beside him. With my arms around him, I spoke into his ear, telling him who I had called, who was on their way, and who had arrived to see him. As people came in, they would talk to him and share their love for him, saying their goodbyes.

Hearing what Clyde had meant to these people, and witnessing their love and support of him, one after another, was heart wrenching and heartwarming all at the same time. The final person to arrive was his cousin, Lynn. Ironically, she and I had never met before that moment, though we had spoken on the phone several times. She was far too upset to speak, beyond an "I love you" as she struggled with her words and the reality of what was taking place in the room. Finally, I whispered in his ear: "Lynn is here. The last person to arrive is here, and we are all together. We are here with you, and we love you. It's okay; you can go now. We are all here to see you off." Then, the nurse in the room, standing beside his equipment, asked if everyone in the room would kindly step outside into the hallway, because she was going to turn off the machines. At the same time, I was telling him it was okay to leave. A few people closest to the door had started to make their way out of the room, when the nurse said: "Stop, you don't have to leave the room."

Then she explained that Clyde had just passed away on his own, so she did not need to turn the machines off. It was so like him to take charge of himself and his environment, as with everything he did. He had believed he would be able to wait until everyone was in the room, and just as we had discussed in the weeks leading up to this day, it happened exactly as he believed it would.

At the funeral, his friend, Jerry, did a beautiful job with the eulogy, and he mentioned that when he and Clyde were children, they had talked about how they wanted to die. Clyde had always told him that he was going to die in the

Clyde's Story: What a High Vibrational Life Looks Like

arms of the woman he loved. Jerry mentioned how lucky Clyde was, because that was exactly how Clyde left.

Clyde was cremated, and following his funeral, his only sister took possession of his remains, keeping their whereabouts private. She has never revealed what she did with his remains, or where his family or I can go and pay our respects.

In the years since, I still feel the same as I did when I first met Clyde. Prior to him and me taking physical form, we had already pre-arranged that we were going to live on this planet for a little time of fifty years, each of us searching out and learning what people think, see, and feel to be true, living in this existence. He was going to approach it from an analytical point-of-view. Here I was, following my instincts from a place of knowing, a place of spirit, which had to be the furthest thing from analytical.

He and I had come at it from two different perspectives: what do people in this world think, believe, and experience from a human perspective, in connection with their inner light, their inner vibration, and their inner Spirit World? Where do they think they come from, and what is their purpose in life? We were going to take notes, and it was almost like a pre-set appointment. Our meeting and collaboration of the mind and heart consisted of one year and three days. I realized that it actually took two individual's separate experiences to learn as much as we did in such a short period of time and pass the knowledge forward as the one living survivor of that knowledge.

After Clyde died, to say that I was having a hard time coping with his passing is an understatement. His loss was life changing and, just as before, during extreme difficult times of change, my vibration lowered, and I temporarily lost my ability to connect with my inner Spirit World and retracted into seclusion. Slowly coming through my loss, I engaged in nurturing activities, such as going for long walks along the lake, eating whole live foods, listening to music, and singing along with the music. Through these activities, I raised my vibration and once again rekindled Clyde's and my relationship. Only this time, we were living in different realms. He used to tease me, saying that because he knew I could communicate through the collective conscious field of vibration, just because he or I died, did not mean that we would be away from each other.

We would simply be with each other in a different way. He continues to provide guidance, direction, and encouragement, and gives me heck when I need to *get a move on*. Knowing I am in the habit of forgetting to take breaks during a work day, I love the way he puts our favorite song, *I'm Yours*, by Jason Mraz, on the radio at the exact moment that he shows up. Coaxing me with his big smile, to get up, he comes over and takes me by the hand, encouraging me to get out of my chair, and we dance together, just like when he was alive.

Although I try to give comfort to other people in addressing the loss of their loved ones, I do understand that the relationship is completely different once the person passes away, because you are not able to physically touch them, to smell their scent, share the love and laughter, and the beauty of the everyday. I try to bring reassurance to other people, just as Clyde does to me, that they are still right here. He still brings love and laughter into my life. I can still feel him hold me, but not on my skin as with a human to human touch, but rather in the energy of the aura that surrounds my body, that makes my body tingle with a sense of awareness that our spirit essence is united. It feels like a soft, gentle breeze washing over me and moving the hair on my skin. I feel him hold my energy, my place in this world, in the same way as all our loved ones do, to let us know that we are not alone, and that they are still with us—which is only one of the amazing benefits I experience, and you can as well.

I never studied religion as a subject or as a means to explore world history. I was raised under the Roman Catholic Church and understand that what I was encouraged to believe in was in conflict with my experiences with the Spirit World. Clyde had studied religions throughout the planet, and he came to the same conclusion: There is a God, a creator of the seen and unseen living realms, and we are all the children of the Creator.

During the church services I attended, the Priest, reading from the Bible, preached that: "Christ will come again to judge the living and the dead." I have to say that these words have never resonated with me as feeling quite right. I do believe Christ will come again! But not to judge the living and the dead. My vision looks a little different. What if Christ's return to earth is not in human form at all? What if the return of God, here on earth, is actually us coming into our full awakening that we are God's children, and realizing we have the ability to raise our current unified vibration to the heightened extent that we create the God consciousness here on earth? What if *we* are the returning Christ we have been waiting for? To these questions, I am comfortable with the answer: "Yes! I believe we have the ability to raise our personal and unified consciousness, our God vibration, and as we do, we will discover we have the ability to repeat the same miracles as described in the Bible and create more of our own."

Most of this book is written as if there are two separate worlds—not because I believe that but to help me to describe which realm of consciousness I am referring to. There is no overlap but rather one reality with different perspectives. We are all connected, and our living vibration is at the core of who we are. We are the Creator's children, and we are here to create!

Keep in mind, the Spirit World is not another place, the way we think of going from one city to another or traveling to a different country. It is who we are. We are living spirits, having a human experience. Referring to the Spirit World as a separate place helps others to firstly become familiar with the concept that there is such a place, to understand what is possible, and give clarity to what abilities lie dormant, waiting to be discovered within them when they choose to expand beyond their current beliefs and their five senses, and to live each moment in full awareness, being open to their undiscovered possibilities. We are all raised with different belief systems. We are all the same energy—spirit beings— having a human experience in a temporary suit, called a body, that contributes to our collective human experience, as a result of being a unified living vibration. As my father-in-law discovered and reported back to me after passing, he did not have to believe in a much larger existence beyond his death: "It just is." The good news is that you do not have to die to come to this realization!

For me to attempt to explain this concept to you, and have you discover it for yourself, I first must have you recognize and understand that there is more living to be created and experienced beyond your physical form and five senses. Where you find yourselves today is in distinct relation to your personal thoughts, your belief in the probability of those thoughts coming into fruition, your ability to visualize interactions and relationships, or lack thereof that led up to this moment.

My grief over losing Clyde made me less inclined to explore a new relationship, but Clyde reached out to me and told me that it was time to find my next partner, and directed me to look on a specific website, one that had helped me to connect with Clyde. It had only been five months, and I did not feel ready, but Clyde kept pushing, so I activated my profile and, again, used the keyword, *aura*.

This is where I met Jack. Of course, I needed validating information from the universe that this was going to be my next partner. In the course of our discussion about where we were from, and those basic details about our lives, we found that our paths had crossed for one year in junior high. On our first date, Jack brought out the school yearbook. There we were in all our geeky glory. When I saw his photo from back then, I remembered his energy and passing him in the hallways. I remembered exactly who he was.

Our date consisted of dinner at Snug Harbour on the shores of Lake Ontario. After dinner, I asked if he would like to go for a walk with me and Lucy who had been patiently waiting in the car. It was dark, and as we approached one of the street lights, it went out. The ability to affect streetlights is something I discovered about myself as a teenager, and is referred to as a SLIder. The SLI stands for "street lamp interference."

I was panicking inside but keeping it cool on the outside. I kept telling myself that I needed to calm my energy, because I was blowing street lights. At the same time, I hoped that he would not connect it to me, because street lights go out all the time. But by the third one, Jack was becoming a bit suspicious that there was something more to it. He stopped walking, and he looked down at me. "Is there something you want to tell me?" It was a pregnant pause, and I did not know what to say. "I'm nervous." Then his face softened up, and he said: "I thought it was you. There is no need to be nervous." He held out his hand, and our energies connected as we held hands. I felt the calm of the moment, and my nervousness dissipated. I knew that this was where I was supposed to be, and this was my next partner.

Now, I had two men sharing in my life. Clyde from the spirit side, and Jack on the physical side. Both were very supportive as I was building my business and choosing the next direction for my journey.

Clyde's Story: What a High Vibrational Life Looks Like

I do not claim to be technologically savvy, and seeing that Clyde was a computer genius, I find myself asking him for help with computer questions, and he guides me through. As humans, we occasionally have a need to ask for help, and it does not have to be limited to those who are still with us in a physical form. Those who have passed on and are now living in spirit can help us as well. We just have to ask.

With music playing in the background, and a boisterous laugh, I always knew when Clyde was in the room. It was how he held his energy, not afraid of giving his all in everything he did, which included his openness to being strong and confident with his choices, yet vulnerable when shedding a tear while watching a movie or empathizing and supporting a friend in pain. He lived his life to the absolute fullest, and one of his favorite sayings that he often presented me with was: "When *now* would you like to do that?"

I met his cousin, Lynn, at the hospital. She and I had said that we would like to get know each other personally. She had an event through work and invited me to come and check out the farmer's market where her company had a booth. I brought Lucy along.

When I arrived, there was something about the vendors offering their wares around her booth and during various events throughout the day, which held a strong sense of familiarity. It was as if Clyde was spending the day with us. It made sense, though, because we were becoming friends due to our connection through Clyde.

Just out of view from her booth, there was live music playing throughout the day, with the entertainers changing every forty-five minutes. Just as we were talking about Clyde, sharing a mutual feeling that he was with us, a bagpiper began to play Amazing Grace, which was played at his funeral.

During Clyde's service, the Dragon Boat team raised and joined the tips of their paddles to form an arch, under which his casket passed, both entering and exiting the funeral. As the paddles were raised, and Clyde's remains exited the room, followed by the guests, they were accompanied by the sounds of bagpipes playing Amazing Grace, which echoed throughout the halls of the funeral home. It was at this moment I discovered that Lynn does not believe in coincidence either, and said it was a sign confirming Clyde was truly with us and that he approved of our efforts to begin a friendship.

Once I was ready to leave, Lynn, her son, and her son's friend were kind enough to walk Lucy and me back to my car to see us off. As we walked to my car, it was her son that said he felt as if Clyde was walking with us, which Lynn and I admitted that we felt it too.

Finally, we reached my car, and I loaded Lucy into the back seat. We said goodbye, and then, as I started my car to leave, I noticed that an apple I had left in the cup holder between the seats, had a bite taken out of it. Instantly, I heard Clyde say, "Show Lynn. She will know what this means."

When I picked it up, the apple looked like it had three small bites taken out of it, each the approximate size of a nickel, which gave it the appearance of one larger bite. Given that the apple was in a locked car for half a day, knowing I had placed it in my cup holder in immaculate condition, I was shocked to see it had changed its appearance in such a perfect formation. I jumped out of the car, with Lucy in tow, and caught up with Lynn at her booth. I showed her the apple and said: "This was in my car." She put her open hand to her chest. Her eyes filled up with tears, and she told me that it was a message from Clyde, and that he was here.

Then, Lynn told me about a Neil Diamond CD, with the song, *One More Bite of the Apple.* Prior to Clyde and me meeting, on one of Clyde's visits to her home, she played her then new CD for him. When he had heard that song, he had her play it a few more times and ended up borrowing the CD. But it never made it back to Lynn. Eventually, she ended up buying a new one, and told him to keep it.

He talked to her about that song so much that it was ingrained in her mind as a link to Clyde. I then took the apple to another friend, Leslie, who also had that ingrained in her mind as a Clyde song. She believed that would have been the number one way he would have presented himself, if he was with us. We ended up making impressions of the apple with candle wax, and the images of those impressions are illustrated below.

Clyde's Story: What a High Vibrational Life Looks Like

The apple in the car with Clyde's bite.

Wax impression of Clyde's apple bite is forming.

Living Supernatural in the Natural World

Wax impression of Clyde's apple bite.

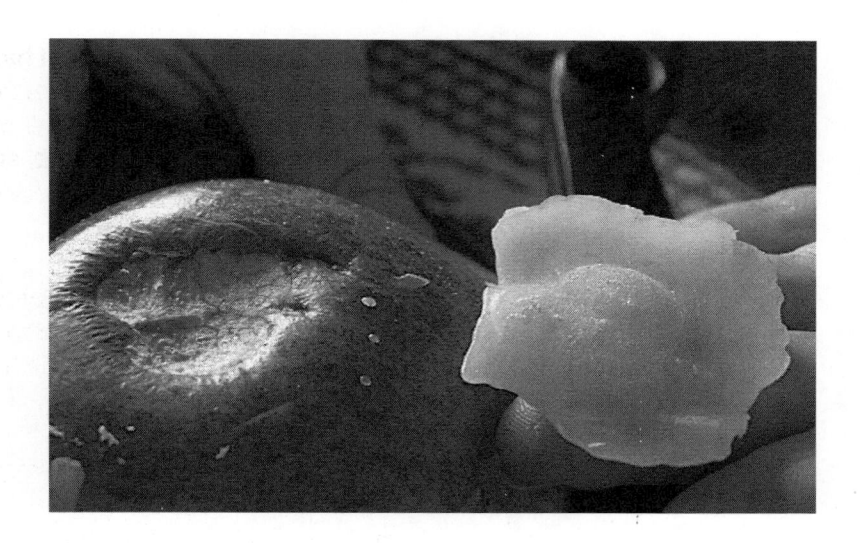

Clyde's Story: What a High Vibrational Life Looks Like

When Clyde was alive, he discovered he was able to manifest his desires into his physical life through his intentions, affirmations, and vision boards. Since his passing, he has equally illustrated his ability to manifest his desires directly from spirit into physical form, as validated in his being able to take a bite out of my apple.

This was not to be the end of Clyde's ability to communicate and create. On another occasion, Jack and I went to the United States on a weekend retreat, with the primary purpose of digging for crystals in an Arkansas mine. Most of the participants were from the United States and had their own cars. We had a rented car, so when we left the hotel in the mornings to go to the mine site, we traveled together as a convoy rather than renting a bus.

Among the participants, there was a woman who was also from Canada, named Myrna; so, along with Jack and me, that made three Canadians in the group. Naturally, when she needed a ride, we offered, and she jumped into the backseat of our car. The three of us immediately hit it off, becoming good friends over the course of the weekend.

During one of the trips together, Myrna piped up from the backseat: "I have someone here named Boom, and he's really talkative." This was Clyde's last name, which was very unusual. Taken completely by surprise by her announcement, I turned and said: "You're a medium." She confirmed it, and Jack told her that he must be here for Diane. "No, he's here for you, Jack," said Myrna.

She gave Jack a message from Clyde. Part of his message was that he wanted to have a beer with Jack. Clyde wanted him to sit down, open two beers, and through mind-to-mind communication, they would have a conversation. "Tell him I will take him up on his offer, and I'll book it into my schedule," said Jack.

By Clyde talking to Myrna, it was the perfect way for Clyde to introduce himself to Jack. Myrna gave many verifying details and described Clyde to a tee, but she had no idea who Boom was. There was no possible way that she would have known he was my previous partner who had passed away. Boom was not a common name, but it was a name I had called Clyde in the past.

One of the things that Clyde and I were in the habit of doing was having deep conversations, lying on the bed and facing each other with our hands clasped, with our energies intertwined and connected. When Jack and I started our relationship, I asked him if he was interested in carrying on this ritual with me. We did carry on that tradition, but one day, when we were talking, Clyde interjected. He just popped into my head and started speaking to me through mind-to-spirit communication, known as mediumship. So, I was carrying on two conversations: one with Clyde in the Spirit World, and one with Jack in the physical world. Then, Clyde told me that he was learning to do new things between the spiritual and physical, and wanted to show me. As Jack was speaking, Clyde manifested ectoplasma, and superimposed his face over Jack's, while I was still having these two conversations. Clyde, due to his playful nature, was excited to show me what he could do. I was giggling a bit on the inside. With Jack, I was trying to not let on what was happening to his face from the spirit realm.

Ectoplasma is a transparent gel-like substance that is most commonly known as the matter that emanates from the body of a spiritualistic medium during communication with the dead, with which I am familiar and have had experience with. Jack is not a medium, nor was he aware of what was happening.

Although I was enjoying it, I asked Clyde to stop, but he told me that he could do more. The next thing was changing Jack's voice to sound like Clyde's, by manipulating Jack's vocal cords. On one hand, this was funny, but on the other hand, I was in an intimate setting with my new partner, while sharing a moment with my previous partner. Hearing his voice, I went from giggling in my head to breaking down. I really missed Clyde, and for him to be able to that was a double-edged sword.

I was seeing the spirit of both men at that moment. While I was excited for Clyde, I told him I missed him too much for him to keep doing that. It was too much for me emotionally. He stopped immediately, because he did not realize how it would affect me. He just thought it would be fun, and it was fun for a moment. But the impact was much greater than either of us could have anticipated.

Clyde's Story: What a High Vibrational Life Looks Like

Jack could see that something had happened, because the conversation I had been having with him could not have had such an emotional impact. I was even rubbing my throat because I had such a big lump in it and had a hard time speaking. He asked me if I was okay, and I shared what had just happened. This led Jack and I to have a conversation about how difficult it is to have a relationship when the other man he is competing with is not in a body.

Jack was not upset in the sense of being angry, but he genuinely asked the question of how he could compete with someone he could not see, and he never knew when Clyde would show up. I told him to leave that with me and that we would figure it out.

After we had returned from our crystal mining trip, Jack booked time in his planner to go home early and meet with Clyde. He opened two beers, setting one in front of him and one in front of the empty chair beside him. During their conversation, Jack made a special request of Clyde: when it was a private moment of any kind, even if it was just a private conversation, he asked that Clyde not come to me during that time. They reached an understanding of sorts on how to share me, a person who is very special to them both.

One other request was that Clyde not superimpose his face over Jack's anymore, and Clyde has also honored that request. Jack felt that Clyde agreed to that. Although he could not hear Clyde, Jack received a sense of protectiveness about me. His role was to take care of me and make sure that I was okay. I have a journey to fulfill, as we all do, and part of Jack's journey was to be by my side to help me through those encounters, and to be there as part of my support system. Jack verbally agreed to take care of me. That was their conversation over a beer. Since we met, Jack is increasingly learning to trust his intuition.

Clyde showed me how he could create, and hold molecules together, using plasma to superimpose his face over Jack's. Just as when you were born, he entered into physical form as a creator of pure consciousness, vibrating energy, and came from what appeared to be nothingness, emanating from a human egg the size of a grain of sand, and sperm that could swim on the head of a pin. He is a high vibrating master, fully capable of creating his environment in all realms of consciousness in which he lives, as are you.

Clyde used these skills to mentor me as I recovered through those years I suffered with PTSD following my car accident, the Spirit World remained active and alive; it was I who had disconnected myself from reaching it. I removed myself from that part of me, because fear lowered my vibration, and I temporarily lost sight of my inner spirit. I needed to remove that fear and remind myself of who I really was, by rebuilding my self-esteem and self-confidence. It was not an easy road, because this is not the kind of thing I would typically share with someone else. How could I tell another human being that I could no longer connect with a larger, invisible world that when connected puts me in a perfect state of knowing, and without it, I was frightened?

Today, I am living my purpose by being a mentor for others. I am the person who totally understands what you are going through on your journey.

Throughout this chapter, I have discussed examples of how to create your physical reality through your beliefs, affirmations, and vision boards; feeling isolated from the Spirit World; mediumship; using plasma; and signs from those who have passed. I also demonstrated how someone who did not have a background in these types of connections—Jack—was able to raise his vibration to begin to explore his own ability.

We, as a society, have become very individualized. Rather than going with the natural flow of life and allowing our collective vibration to rise as we recognize and accept the unity that we are, just like Siamese twins share one heart, we are feeling the strain of trying to separate ourselves as individuals while being perfectly connected.

The perspective we need to come from is: "What can I do to be a better person?" and "What can I do to better serve the collective and myself?"

Information is great, but the frequency is more important, as that is where the transformation takes place! Would you like to live the mind-blowing, fulfilled life you were meant to live? Would you like to know what you can do that will instantly raise your vibration and make a massive difference in the quality of your life?

Clyde's Story: What a High Vibrational Life Looks Like

Try this! Eat live, non-processed food, and drink non-chemical, non-chlorinated clean water, out of a glass container. Use non-fluoridated toothpaste. Use biodegradable soap, shampoo, conditioner, body creams, lotions, and makeup. Sing, dance, play, and listen to high vibrational music, and for goodness sake, stop listening to what the media has to say about the fearful world they portray. Miracles happen every day; look for them, as what we focus on, grows! Disengage from gossip, fabricated truths, and your WAG. Yes, your *Wild Ass Guess* of a situation that creates drama and lowers your vibration. Release your rigid, analytical thoughts, and engage in free-flowing, creative activities, such as colouring, swimming, sports, or do-it-yourself projects. As your vibration rises to a more heightened state, you will begin to live in a complete state of knowing the truth of any situation, without feelings of judgment toward the situation.

Get outside in nature. Stop isolating yourself! Get involved in a community where you engage in activities that bring you joy, and togetherness that serves others. Yes, it can get messy! Start working on your shit! Engaging with family and community has a way of bringing up all of your stuff and gives you the opportunity to work through the things that need to be worked through more quickly. All through the beauty of...messing up. Often.

You are the powerful Creator's child! Rise to the occasion of what it truly means to be that child and create your reality...with love.

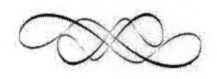

Chapter 9

They Said Nothing Happened – They Lied

We had been married for five years, had two children, and we were long overdue for an intimate get away. After discussing the idea with our parents, we decided to take a trip to Jamaica, just the two of us. The two sets of grandparents had decided that they would each take one child for a week, and then they would switch, so they would each get to spend time with each grandchild separately during the two weeks of our being away.

As the date of departure approached, in preparation for the trip, I started packing for each child. My two-year-old had been given a two-piece suit with a bow tie, which made him look like a mini-version of a businessman. Totally engrossed in the process of putting aside what would be needed, without thought, I automatically included his suit. When my husband came in the room to see how I was making out, he noticed the suit amongst the clothing to be packed, and asked: "What is this doing in here?"

Without skipping a beat, my automatic response was: "For the funeral."

My husband looked at me with a funny expression because he did not know of any services planned while we were going to be away, and asked: "Whose funeral?" It was not until he asked me that question, that I paid attention to what I had said, and responded: "I don't know. But there is going to be a funeral, and he is going to need it." He pointed out, if there were such a service, then the family would arrange for a sitter to watch the boys. They would not take them to a funeral, since they were both so young. I agreed with his reasoning, and the little suit came out of the case.

The first few days in Jamaica were heaven on earth. The people were warm and welcoming, the weather was amazing, and we were cramming as much in as we possibly could in that amazing paradise. One night, during our first week, I woke up with a vision that came through in the form of a dream. It appeared from the perspective of a bird's eye view, hovering over a street intersection. It was night, and the halos of the street lights, along with the sheen on the road, indicated that it had rained, and it had been raining for some time.

There was a peaceful silence in the air as I watched the traffic lights taking turns changing from green, to yellow, to red. There was no one in sight, and as I took in my surroundings, I was drawn to a set of equally spaced embedded tracks on the ground. They resembled railroad tracks that started roadside and led off into a grassy field. At the end of these tracks, I saw what appeared to be a singular boxcar of a train that was set alight, off into the distance.

I was at a loss to understand what I was looking at, but the message that accompanied it was perfectly clear: something was terribly wrong. I woke my husband up and shared my vision. My husband listened to my vision and, after hearing me out, he held me, and we both drifted back to sleep.

Later that same night, I was awakened again, startled and taking in a big gasp of breath. It was so intense that it woke my husband up as well. He asked what had happened, and I told him that it was the same vision, but I now knew the boxcar was not a boxcar at all, and it was not abandoned. It was now surrounded by police cars, an ambulance, and fire trucks, with pylons set up to redirect traffic. The road and field were now a hub of activity. The area was so brightly lit up from all the lights, trucks, and cars, that it was as if I were a hovercraft directly above the scene.

This time, I received the message that someone had passed over. They were telling me how it happened by means of this vision. I shared all this with my husband, including details about how the accident occurred. Drawing pictures, I explained that the driver had lost control of the vehicle on the wet slick road and had hit and driven over a street sign that punctured the undercarriage of the tank, and came to rest in the field. What I had originally interpreted as railroad tracks were actually the impressions in the field created by the tires of the car, and the reason they were so pronounced was due to the saturated soil from the rain.

They Said Nothing Happened – They Lied

I was up the rest of the night, as I kept asking the Spirit World for more information. As I started to doze, half awake and half asleep, I saw a vision of my aunt and uncle's home, with the police coming to give them the sad news of my cousin's terrible accident. I could feel my aunt's emotions of loss and devastation. I saw them crying and pacing in disbelief. There was so much turmoil in their home, and there was nothing I could do for them but feel their pain.

I woke up from my sleep, crying. As I told my husband what was going on, he came up with a plan. We would wait for it to be a reasonable time at home; then we would call and check in with my family to find out what, if anything, had happened.

Later that morning, I called my mother and told her my feeling that something terrible had happened, that there had been an accident during the night. I asked if everything was okay, and if she had received any phone calls from the family. She said everything was fine. I asked about the children, and my mother assured me that all was well. With that reassurance, my husband and I went off to enjoy the day's activities. But throughout the day, I continued to receive flashes, letting me know that phone calls were being made, and my family was gathering.

I told my husband that my mother was wrong—something had happened—because phone calls were being made, and members of my extended family were starting to receive those phone calls. Plane reservations were being made for people to come into town for the funeral. I could feel these events and the pain behind them.

My husband didn't know what to make of it. He had shared many of my experiences with the Spirit World, but this was unique in comparison to anything that had occurred before in our relationship. While he might have heard about experiences at this level, he had never been through one with me before where I had received such clear information from the Spirit World, and he was unsure what to do.

Think about it for a moment. His mother-in-law was telling him everything was fine, while I was telling him everything was not fine. But I had no physical evidence that my mother was not being honest. I am sure that on one level, he was wondering if I was beginning to crack up. After every phone call home, I was unsettled and adamant that my cousin had passed, and there had been a horrible tragedy, but my mother kept reassuring us that everything was fine. In a way, I felt sorry for my husband, because looking back, the rest of our vacation could not have been much fun for him. I was an emotional wreck, grieving a loss that I had no confirmation of; and yet I knew it had taken place. It definitely was cramping our relaxing vacation style. While he wanted me to put it out of my mind, I couldn't. I kept feeling everyone's grief and sadness, as if I was right there with them. Like a snowball at the top of the mountain that grows larger and larger as it rolls down the mountainside, my emotions seemed to grow bigger and bigger as the days passed. I was trying to make sense of the information I was receiving from the Spirit World, which was not being validated in our physical world.

The day of my cousin's funeral, I was an emotional wreck. Here I was, on one of the most beautiful islands on our planet, and I could not stop crying. The two worlds were in disagreement with each other. The Spirit World had given me a clear picture of what was happening on another continent, but my family was telling me something entirely different. It was extremely confusing and upsetting. My husband thought I was losing my mind, because I was contradicting everything we were being told from home. Each day, I was giving him very specific details of what was going on at home, from the planning stages of the funeral to the day of the funeral itself.

Everything that happened, as it was happening, I would describe it to him. Finally, I said to myself, this isn't fair to my husband. We had not had a vacation, and I wanted to make this a pleasurable trip for him. But my grief at times overwhelmed me because I wanted to be with my family, honor my cousin's life, and take part in supporting my family.

We flew home on a red-eye flight. My mother-in-law came to pick us up at the airport. We were going to spend the night at my in-laws before heading to our home with the children. At least, that had been the plan. When we arrived at her home, we had tea and coffee, sharing our two-week experience and all the fun it had been. Now, if things had gone according to plan, I knew which child was supposed to be at her home. When I asked where they were sleeping and if I could go and peek in on that child, she told me that the plans had changed, and both children were with my parents.

They Said Nothing Happened – They Lied

She made up a story about how the two-year-old had kept asking for us and his brother, so they thought it was better that they be together for the last few days. The next day, we planned to go and get the children from my parents. I said that it had been a long day, and then I excused myself and went to bed. Gary decided to spend some time with his mother and said he would join me shortly. After they thought that I was asleep, my mother-in-law told my husband about my cousin's car accident, and that he would have to share the bad news with me in the morning. He was shocked to hear that something had happened while we were away and asked for details. His first thought was for the children, but my mother-in-law reassured him that they were fine.

Then she shared that my cousin had died in an accident during the first week that we were away. Gary just stared at his mother in total disbelief. Here I had been telling him all these details, which he thought indicated I was going crazy, but in fact, I had been right. His mother had just confirmed it.

He told his mother: "Diane already knows." My mother-in-law did not think it was possible, but as Gary shared the details that I had told him, his mother confirmed that it was exactly what had happened. Then she shared information with him, and he confirmed that it matched with what I had said happened. The sequence of events and when they happened were also accurate.

After all this information had been shared between them, Gary asked why no one had told us. He said that I kept calling home, and everyone told me that everything was fine. My mother-in-law shared that they had discussed it as a family and decided that they would not tell me, so that I could enjoy my trip with Gary. They knew if I had been told, I would have wanted to come home immediately to be with the family, and they wanted us to enjoy this special trip.

As a result, while they had tried to spare me the grief and protect me, I had been going through it alone, without any family around me. It was an isolating experience, to say the least. Their plan had backfired, and my husband had been alone with me, thinking I was losing my mind. Good intentions were in play, but they had decided without consulting me.

This meant that for the first week, Gary's parents had the children, and my family was able to take them for the second week. This allowed my family to focus on the arrangements and the needs of the family during the funeral preparation, as well as taking care of family that came in from out of town for the service.

I don't think Gary slept at all that night after his discussion with his mother. His face was pale, and it looked as if he had not moved from the kitchen table all night. The same cup of coffee was in front of him when I entered the kitchen the next morning. Our eyes met, and I knew he was upset. So, I asked him what was wrong, and why hadn't he come to bed. I just wanted him to say it fast, but he had me sit down and held my hand. Then he told me that my cousin, Michael, had passed.

In a way, I felt vindicated; I wasn't crazy after all! But as he confirmed that all the details I had shared with him in Jamaica matched with what had occurred, I broke down. My husband held me as I cried. All the messages I had received from the Spirit World were being confirmed. Of course, then I had the same question as my husband, "Why had everyone lied to me? Why?"

This was a question that I felt could only be answered by my mother, because she had been the one who deceived me through every phone call, when I called home. We drove to my parents' home, and she could tell by the expression on my face that I knew what had happened. I was upset by the loss of my cousin, and disappointed in her for not telling the truth. We hugged, and then I asked her why the secrecy; why the lies? She shared her reasons, which came from a place of love. She wanted us to enjoy our vacation and time together without dwelling on this tragic news, and thought if she had told me, I would have come home immediately, which she felt would not have been fair to me or Gary. She also thought I should find out when we were together as a family, instead of all by myself on an island far from home.

I shared that the decisions she made on my behalf were not hers to make, and I should have been told the truth from the start. I reminded her that she had been the one demanding I ignore my intuition and the information the universe provides, and how ironic it was that she turned out to be the one person who taught me to trust it the most!

No matter what my family may have intended, the experience had been emotionally painful. Instead of sharing the experience with my family, I experienced his death, the planning of, and his actual funeral service, one hundred percent through the eyes of the Spirit World. The human touch, that connection with my family, the tradition of gathering together sharing stories, supporting, and expressing our love to one another, and to Michael, was what I had missed out on. It was important to me that I be there with them, and when we got back, everyone was gone, and there was no closure for me.

I went back to work and carried on with my life, but I still felt the lack of closure. Throughout my life, I have one overriding belief, which is that there are no coincidences. Everything happens for a reason. That being said, as I traveled back and forth to work, each day I passed the cemetery that Michael was buried in. In the mornings, I would say: "Good morning, Michael, how are you this beautiful day?" I would spend the time keeping him up to date on what was happening with our family members. On my way home, I would repeat the process of saying hello, and then share how my day went.

Eventually, he answered. Excited to hear from him, we talked about what happened with his accident. I then told him that I did not know where he was in the cemetery because I had been in Jamaica when he passed. So, he invited me into the cemetery and said he would show me where he was. I followed his directions and eventually reached the spot in one of the large open grass sections that was dusted with snow on the ground. This snow made it difficult to see the headstones that were embedded and flush to the ground.

After following his directions, I could not find his name plate. I was now standing in what appeared to be a grassy field, crusted with a light layer of snow. I bent down to move it aside, hoping to reveal his plaque. No matter how precisely I tried to follow his directions, I became frustrated that I could not locate his name plate. He told me to stand up, where to place my feet, and in what direction to face. He then told me to lift and extend my arms parallel to my shoulders, straight out from my sides, and to open the palm of my hands. There I stood, with completely open arms, and he told me: "I'm right in front of you between your fingertips." Again, I got on my knees to break away the crusty snow, to no avail. I could not find him.

I told him I would be back, and then I headed home and called my mother. I explained the situation and asked her to come with me the next day to help me locate his head stone. She agreed and met me at the cemetery gates, got in my car, crossed her arms, and said, "Show me." So, I followed my cousin's directions through the large cemetery, following all the twists and turns of the roads he directed me to take, and once again stopped my car where he instructed me to park. We got out of the car and walked along the aisles amongst the burial plots, and I took her to the spot as directed.

Now, standing with my arms extended once more, she searched the ground and could not find his identifying plaque either. She told me to stay still, and I watched as she took my car and drove to a large building on the premises in the distance. When she returned, she had a map of the cemetery that explained the cemetery grounds as a grid, along with the longitude and latitude numbers, written on a separate piece of paper, indicating Michael's location. Together, we read the map, found his location, and compared it to where we were standing. We came to the same conclusion, that Michael was directly in front of me, at my feet. Although we could not find any markings to confirm his name, the grid map of his immediate neighbors did confirm that he was laid to rest in that spot. We never did find his plaque.

This gave my mother and me another opportunity to have a deep discussion about this ability that we both had developed to communicate with the Spirit World, and the loving guidance that we could receive from that source.

After this experience, I continued to talk with my cousin, but now, instead of releasing his energy before I went home, I took it with me. This opened a door to other spirits, which seemed to create a party atmosphere in my home. My cousin did not know them, and I wanted to know why they were here. It felt like a party line of sorts, but I wanted to find out why they were coming to me. I had never experienced anything of this magnitude before, and I was trying to make sense of the situation.

Most of the spirits were fun and friendly, and I enjoyed getting to know them as they came and went. Some of these spirit contacts became very persistent. They were unwilling to leave because they wanted me to contact their loved ones. They had messages that they wanted me to deliver. Up to that point in my life, I had not shared messages with strangers from their loved ones residing in spirit. It had always been immediate family and close friends.

This situation was getting out of hand, and because it was new to me, I did not know how to handle persistent spirits that would not leave my home. So, I asked Michael for advice on how to handle it. He confirmed that they wanted me to be a spokesperson and pass messages along to their friends and families. The problem was, I was reluctant to do so. I had my own life to live, and I was not sure I was ready to add this to the mix. One spirit in particular was a strong energy that did not appreciate me saying no to the idea of delivering his message.

I had to get this situation under control, so Michael and I stopped communicating at my home, and went back to our conversations during my commute to and from work. My sending a clear intention out to the universe that spirits were to stay outside my home, seemed to be the beginning of the clearing of my home from other spirits. One by one, the spirits left as they realized I was not going to do what they wanted, and they abided by my decision—except for the one strong spirit. It was simply not going to leave until I did what it wanted, which I was not willing to do.

As a result, strange things started to occur in our home. I would see flashes of light from the spirit, out of the corner of my eye. Or hear the slow squeaking motion of the wood floor boards as though someone was walking on the living room floor and the staircase that led to the bedrooms, even though no one was there. Small items, such as hair brushes, spoons, and pens, would be visible one moment and gone the next. It was annoying and playful all at the same time. It became a war of wills, because as the spirit became more assertive in exercising its ability to transform the physical realm, I got angrier and more unwilling to comply. Then it started to affect my children's wellbeing. One of the main issues was that my children were being woken up at night with an unknown entity in their room. They would sense a presence in their room and call my name to see if it was me. Keeping the lights off in and outside their room, I would come to their doorway to respond to their calling my name. Time and again they would ask if I had just been in their room. When I answered, "No," they would respond: "Then who was?"

I would then enter their room and slide in beside them by sitting at the head of their bed to gently answer their questions, such as: "Did you see them?" We would then review their experience, covering various topics, such as: "What did the energy feel like? Were they happy, playful, scary, calm, or neutral? Did they feel the presence in the room? Or did they actually see them with their eyes, or in their mind's eye? What did they look like? Are they still here? Did they speak to you?" If so: "What did they say?"

While my children were never confronted by the spirit entity, they did not like the feeling that someone was in their room and would not reveal themselves, and they wanted it to stop. We had several discussions about the Spirit World, their experience, how they felt, and the importance of them setting boundaries. My questions included asking them if they felt safe. I wanted them to trust their own instincts.

I reassured them that they could call me anytime, and not only would I come to them, I reassured them that I would take care of it. In the meantime, I was discussing the situation with my husband, Gary. I wanted to get his blessing to contact the church and have an exorcism performed on our home. He reminded me that I had been the one who invited the spirits into our home, and it was up to me to get rid of them. It had gotten pretty bad, because neither I nor my children were getting much sleep at night. Gary's determination that I should be the one to take care of this disruptive spirit was the best thing that could have ever happened to me.

I became protective of my family, and over the course of the evening, while lying in bed after responding to my children being woken up by the disruptive spirit yet again, I was determined this would be the last night my family would be disturbed.

Once my family had gone back to sleep, I went into a deeply-centered, high-vibrational meditative state. I visualized my body as being one with my home, and with my mind's voice, I spoke directly to the energy of the brick, mortar, walls, and content. I told it we were going to have a calm, loving, exciting, and happy home, with high vibrational energy. As I experienced the vibration of my body rise, I felt anchored, weightless, powerful, strong, and connected to the universe.

They Said Nothing Happened – They Lied

Our home consisted of five levels. In my mind's eye, starting in the lower basement, I focused on, and saw each room and staircase as through I were actually there. As I created this visual, I was acutely aware that I was also feeling the experience within my body and was connected as a participant. I stayed focused on my intention to relieve my home of this heavy disturbing energy as I systematically walked my thoughts through each room, hallway, and stairwell of my home, all the while clearing the existing energy from the walls and objects in each room, leaving a radiating bright light behind, brighter than the brightest star.

I had now arrived at the dining room, one floor beneath the bedroom level. I felt the lower vibrational energy resist my clearing intentions, and I was being challenged to see which energy would transform first, theirs or mine.

This is when my momma-bear attitude to protect my cubs reared its ugly head. As I mentioned, my home had squeaky dining room floors and a staircase that led to the upper bedroom level. I could now hear the dining room floor start to squeak as the spirit was moving through my home. It started picking up the pace, and I started to taunt it with instructions to get out; so, it got louder, and I got more determined that it was going to leave, tonight! I could feel it getting angrier, and the squeaking on my dining room floor got faster and faster now, sounding more like a jogger running through my house. Round and round, it went through my dining room, living room, and back again, getting faster and louder as it stirred up its rage and resistance.

For the first time ever, I felt threatened for my life, so I jumped out of bed and ran to the top of the stairs and accepted its challenge to come and get me. I could now hear the pounding squeaks on the dining room floor as it went around and around the room until, in one quick swoosh, the energy came flying up the staircase toward me, hitting every step, making a noise similar to running your fingernails across the surface of a chalkboard. I braced myself for the hit, and as it entered my body, I instinctively raised my arms up over my head and, through my mind's eye, shot it through an opening of pure white light back into the universe and out of my home. All I could see in my mind's eye was the clear open universe above me. I threw it in that direction, with the message screaming in my head for it to stay out! In a split second, it was all over. Now, standing at the top of the stairs, the vibrating light within me and my surroundings dissipated, and the darkness of the night came back into my home.

The silence of the night was calming and peaceful, with a soft angelic feel to the air. Then I heard the music. It was a unique instrument that I have never been able to recognize, that played a tune. I tried to find out where it was coming from, but it only played for about sixty seconds. Wherever I went in my home, it was the same volume. I could not locate the source. The next night, while I had no spirit to contend with, the music played again. This music played the same tune and volume each night, at different time intervals, for over two complete years. My children, even as adults today, still remember that music as it floated throughout our home at night, and the source of the music remained a mystery. We all agreed the music did not come from any one location but was coming equally from everywhere throughout the five levels of our home. Eventually, it just stopped. While we were able to get a recording of the music, it did not survive the multiple moves since that time.

Setting boundaries in either realm does not mean you found the secret formula to side-step challenges. What it does do, however, is allow you to proclaim your position to the universe, and have a voice in what you will allow, project from yourself, and participate in. Then you hold firm and watch it materialize.

Throughout my career, I have gone to many homes to determine what kind of energies are within their houses. For those spirits who provide protection, fun, and curiosity to a home, once I have introduced the homeowner to their unexpected guest, and clarified their intentions, many homeowners have chosen to welcome and accept their unique guest as a member of the family. For those spirit energies with less than honorable intentions, I have helped clients to make their environment peaceful and safe once again, by having the spirit move on.

We have the power to set those boundaries. For me, this meant creating a *bouncer*. Much in the way that business owners set guards in place to determine who gets in to their bar, pub or business, I have created clear rules about who in the Spirit World can get through to me. Setting these boundaries is key to letting the Spirit World know what kind of energy I will and will not accept. You can do the same thing.

They Said Nothing Happened – They Lied

For me, any messages coming with love, I am wide open for it. Those that do not come with love, I have my bouncer return that energy back to the sender, with love. I choose not to receive that energy with its negative intentions. This has served me well. Just as we set boundaries in our relationships with others, we can set those same boundaries regarding the energy that we want to have enter from the Spirit World into our physical lives.

Understand that we are dealing with energy; it can never be destroyed but simply changes from form to form. Ouija boards, on the other hand, are quite powerful and do not come with gatekeepers strong enough to screen the energies that come through this board. Erring on the side of caution, playing with a Ouija board is similar to leaving the door to your residence unlocked at night. Without safeguards in place, we do not have control over who comes into our environment. But if you are inclined to receive messages from the Spirit World, there are much safer and easier ways to do so. This includes surrounding yourself with individuals who have experience that can help you do so in a way that is safe, and allows you to set your boundaries effectively.

Chapter 10

Why Increase Your Body Frequency and How?

"Your vibrational frequency determines your experience of life!"

Throughout our lifetimes, we pick up a variety of beliefs, some positive; but others, that are restricting in the way we observe and interact with the world, can hinder our ability to reach our full potential to live a miraculous life. Much like the manager of a go-kart track who has a governor on a go-kart, hindering it from reaching its maximum speed on the race track, we unknowingly have placed a governor on ourselves, which limits our full vibrational potential and life experience.

On one hand, we have what we consider to be our life, and on the other hand, we have what we believe to be our life's meaning. Our life, and our life's meaning, are completely separate from one another. Our bodies have a natural vibrational frequency that the world around us responds to. The higher the vibration, the healthier and more creative we all become, working together as a whole.

The actions that we take, based on our beliefs, are what opens or closes the door to our emotional pain and pleasure responses, which is felt within ourselves, and then radiates out into the world. How we experience our health, our relationships, and even our finances are a direct result of the frequency of our vibration up to this point. When our beliefs become so powerful that they lack the elements of peace, joy, love, compassion, empathy, forgiveness, and gratitude, we are putting a governor around our body's natural vibrations. The results show up in the circumstances of your life!

Mahatma Gandhi was one of the most famous freedom fighters in the history of mankind. He taught Indians to fight for their rights through the path of nonviolence. He led India in its struggle for freedom against British rule and achieved independence on August 15th, 1947.

Although there is some question as to whether or not Mahatma Gandhi actually said these words:

"Be the change you wish to see in the world."

I cannot stress this point enough. This notion of being the change you want to see in the world does three powerful things to raise our unified vibration when we each adopt its message. It draws our attention to stop judging and complaining about others; it opens the opportunity for self-reflection; and stirs us to take action in the realization that the true meaning of power is not in the act of controlling others but lies in the ability to control ourselves.

This powerful message may have been a shortened version of his actual quote, which is equally relevant in our world as vibrational beings having a human experience:

"We but mirror the world. All the tendencies present in the outer world are to be found in the world of our body. If we could change ourselves, the tendencies in the world would also change. As a man changes his own nature, so does the attitude of the world change towards him. This is the divine mystery supreme. A wonderful thing it is and the source of our happiness. We need not wait to see what others do." – Mahatma Gandhi

Have you ever been confronted with stressful situations and people? How you handle these challenges is a direct representation of the frequency you are residing in at that moment. If you are uncertain where you fit on the vibrational scale, simply ask yourself: "Did my response include love?"

When you are willing to transition your thought patterns and actions to a more compassionate level, despite the circumstances, that is when you are well on your way to higher vibrational levels.

Why would you want to raise your frequency? To get unstuck!

Why Increase Your Body Frequency and How?

Your life takes a new direction; it feels complete, uplifted, empowered, and plugged into the physical and nonphysical world, and it is connected in a way you have never experienced up to this moment. You will see and experience the interconnectedness of all life in its miraculous beauty. You will begin to see how you can transition your life for the better and bring amazing miracles into your life and the people around you.

As your frequency increases, so does your sense of *knowing*. You begin to walk, talk, and take action with a higher sense of wisdom, and with an inner compass that will help you fulfill your wildest desires as you create and experience a powerful fulfilled life. You live confidently and speak with a pure sense of knowing; life's purpose becomes clearer, while living with vitality and health.

It will keep you engaged and excited as you explore and discover your ability to turn your perceived low probability belief of the possible, into mind-blowing experiences where the world responds and provides you with what you confidently ask for. To have a high frequency body and mind is to completely understand what it means to be alive in realities you never thought possible—living in full awareness that you are a living energy field, and so is everything and everyone else.

In 1992, Bruce Tainio, of Tainio Technology, built the first frequency monitor in the world, and his findings revealed that low frequencies make undesirable physical changes in the body. Middle frequencies make emotional changes in the body, and high frequencies make spiritual changes in the body. Just as plant seedlings flourish when conditions of sun, water, and soil meet its specific requirements, we flourish in optimal emotional and physical health when our body is resonating above 62 megahertz (MHz), as seen in the chart below, followed by our coming into our spiritual recognition of unity when resonating above 92–360 MHz:

Spiritual frequencies range from: 92–360 MHz
Genius Brain Frequency: 80–82 MHz
Common Brain Frequency: 72 MHz
Brain Frequency Range: 72–90 MHz
Healthy Human Body: 62–78 MHz
Disease starts at: 58 MHz
Colds and Flu start at: 57–60 MHz

Receptive to Cancer at: 42 MHz
Death begins at: 25 MHz

What does Hertz (MHz) mean?
All atoms in the universe have vibrational motion. Each vibrational motion has a *frequency* (the number of oscillations per second), measured in Hertz:

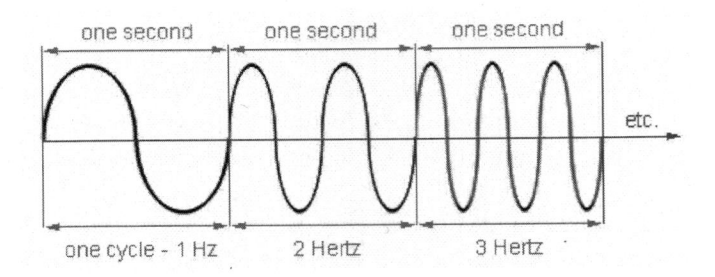

1 Hertz = 1 Hz = 1 oscillation per second
1 Kilohertz = 1 kHz = 1000 oscillations per second
1 Megahertz = 1 MHz = 1,000,000 oscillations per second

15 Simple Ways to Increase Your Body Frequency and Quiet Your Mind

Clearly, there are benefits to increasing your frequency. Below, are 15 ways that you can easily integrate into your life to raise your frequency and find a deeper connection with yourself, as well as with the people and world around you.

1. Laugh for the Fun of It

Raise your energy with lots of laughter by hanging out with high frequency people who love to laugh, are creative in what they say and do, and make you laugh. Find a favorite comedian, or comedians, and follow their shows. Reacquaint yourself with a familiar movie that makes you laugh out loud or do a YouTube search for *silly animals at play*.

Play non-competitive games with friends and family, such as *Pictionary*, which can be played on a large, erasable white board for all to see; or, the game, *Head Bands*, or any game that includes saying silly phrases with a mouth guard and are good for all ages. If it sounds good to you, brings you all together, and makes you laugh, *do it!*

Laughter lives in the higher frequencies; it removes you from the lower frequency energies, where fear, anxiety, and anger live. Laughter raises you to the higher frequencies that connect and empower you to experience the essence of the world and connects you with other high frequency people around you, bringing you all together.

Sunday afternoon has typically been my family's game day, where we excitedly anticipate getting together. The cell phones are turned off; the one-pot dinner is on the back burner of the stove, or only a call away. We all agree outside interruptions are unacceptable as we ...let the games begin!

2. Walk Barefoot Outside – Wear Leather Soled Shoes

Walking barefoot on the grass, on a beach, along the forest floor, or through a garden will allow your body to come into contact with the earth's natural vibrational frequency. This will allow your body to easily release the lower frequencies, giving way to a clear, focused mind, with a calm, relaxed body. When it comes to foot protection, our ancestors had it right when all they wore on the bottoms of their feet were leather soles. Leather, being a natural product, permits the earth's vibration to penetrate through to the bottom of your feet, having the same results as walking barefoot. Rubber and other man-made materials act as a barrier, preventing you from absorbing the earth's natural vibrational energy. Receiving the earth's vibrational energy directly into your body through your feet, increases your health, reduces physical and emotional pain, and provides a calming perspective on the world and your place in it.

3. Eat Raw Organic Foods – Use Essential Oils

Eat raw, organic foods grown in your area, as they have the highest vibrational energy, followed by raw organic foods grown elsewhere. Local farmers markets are ideal as they have the advantage of maintaining the living vibration longer due to their proximity. As we ingest these high vibrational fruits, vegetables, and herbs, they will raise our own vibration levels. Organic or nonorganic, you will never go wrong giving your body raw live foods.

Note: The fresh foods and herbs (megahertz) MHz range listed below can be higher, if grown organically and eaten freshly picked:

Fresh Foods and Herbs: 20–27MHz
Dried Foods and Herbs: 15–22 MHz
Processed/Canned Food: 0 MHz
Therapeutic Grade Essential Oils 52–320 MHz

Every essential oil has a frequency, as do each of our organs and body parts. As there are many uses for essential oils, I encourage you to read up on the importance of essential oils. Seek out an herbalist or a natural foods grocer prior to using any essential oils to determine your needs. They will also be able to help you choose the essential oils that blend well together to accommodate your requests.

Use organic coconut oil. With over 1,500 studies to date, coconut oil is known to be one of the healthiest foods on the planet, and a true superfood. Organic coconut oil can be used in all your cooking and baking requirements, as well as being applied directly on your hair and skin, while providing enormous health benefits.

We have heard the phrase: "We are what we eat." I propose we take a broader look at what it means to achieve and maintain optimal health, which includes "We are what we eat, eats." As well as what we expose ourselves to in every aspect of our lives, and the long-term effects.

4. Explore Rivers and Large Bodies of Water

Visit moving rivers and oceans, with a current, as much as possible.
Yes, immerse yourself in water that has natural movement, as it provides the necessary minerals for improved health! Watch the sunset, or gaze at the waves as they lap onto the shore. Whether you're in it, on it, or beside it, large bodies of water release negative ions that calm the central nervous system, relax your mind, and increase your body's energy frequency.

Why Increase Your Body Frequency and How?

5. Drink Natural Spring Water or Water Taken From a Well

Always ensure you drink plenty of water to help your body flush out the lower vibrational toxins each day. Whenever possible, drink water taken directly from nature. The best would be water derived from a drilled well, filled with minerals. Water has memory. On a molecular level, the same water the dinosaurs drank is sitting in your body at this very moment, connecting you with the earth's vibration since the dawn of time! The earth's filtration system screens through rocks, soil, and sand, and functions in complete harmony with your body as it purifies, gathers, and provides the essential minerals needed to maintain optimal health on all levels. Think outside the box; do you know someone who lives or cottages outside the city limits? You may want to strike up a deal with them for access to their vibration- raising water.

6. Let's Get Physical (((Hugs)))

Get sexual, and experience the big 'O,' often! There is nothing like a good romp in the hay to get mind, body, and spirit in balance and raise your vibration. The fastest way to increase your vibration is through physical contact. Sex and hugs release hormones that make you feel good. Cuddle up with your loved one, a pet, or hug a friend. Close physical contact allows energy transference to occur during contact. By simply being close to each other, energy will be passed from the one with the highest energy vibration to the one with the lower energy frequency, thereby balancing the energy between them. As size has no bearing on the energy transference, even small pets, such as cats and dogs, freely offer their higher energy vibration to their energetically lower or ill vibrating owners. Pets recharge back to their higher vibration through the pads on their feet as they walk outdoor on nature's floor. The happier you feel, the more you will draw happy experiences to yourself because you are operating at a higher frequency.

7. Sing – Play an Instrument – Listen to Music

Sing in the shower, sing in your car, and sing to your heart's content. Each note that you sing, play, or listen to, resonates throughout your body. Singing instantly raises your vibration to the musical note frequencies that your mind, body, and soul will respond to and love you for.

8. Meditation

Meditation begins a process of multi-dimensional actualization through the process of quieting and calming our thoughts away from the mind's chatter, and outside world, bringing it back into the awareness of the moment. All of us can appreciate the benefits of pausing our busy lives to connect with ourselves and take a *time out* to regenerate from the world around us, and reap the benefits of meditation. It will raise you up to fear less and to live more!

Meditation can be as simple as positioning your body in a relaxed and comfortable sitting or lying position. Taking notice of your breath, take in a long, slow breath for the count of five seconds, allowing your mind to shut out all other distractions, then slowly exhale for the count of six seconds. Repeat this process for as little as five minutes, four times a day, or once a day, for 20 minutes or longer.

There are different types of meditations throughout the world. All meditation styles will include most, if not all, of these benefits, with very little variance, so feel free to experiment with different styles. Twenty minutes per day, for a few short weeks, is enough to start experiencing the benefits of meditation. Research has shown that meditation has many mental and physical health benefits. Among other things, it helps reduce depression by 75%, anxiety and stress by 30%, enhances concentration, ignores distractions, and helps manage attention deficit hyperactivity disorder (ADHD).

Meditation improves decision-making, problem-solving, processing of information, memory retention, and recall. It is known to improve sleep, manage pain, and lower blood pressure. Daily meditation practice is ideal for reaping these rewards. In addition, brief mini-meditations can be done as needed throughout the day whenever you want to calm your mind and relax your body.

During meditation you become aware of both your external surroundings and your inner experience, including your own responses to what is going on around you, in the present moment. This experience is referred to as mindfulness.

The goal of mindfulness is to become aware of your surroundings without becoming attached to anything you are experiencing. I highly recommend using mindfulness techniques to combat stressful situations, which can be practiced and achieved during your daily life.

As with all that we do, daily repetition is the key to reaping the benefits of meditation.

9. Gardening – Landscaping and Pottery Making

Just as you receive and increase your vibration from our planet through walking barefoot on the ground, you can also receive it through your hands by doing certain activities, such as gardening, landscaping, pottery making, and building sand castles on the beach.

By taking off the gloves, getting down and dirty in the soil and clay, and handling live minerals, you will absorb their living vibration, which in turn will bring you out of your head into the moment, and increase your vibration while you create an amazing environment and work of art.

10. Exercise Vigorously – Mindful Movement

Dance, play ball in the yard, go for a bike ride, run up and down the stairs, jog or power walk around the neighbourhood. Your body loves it when you move. Make it simple, clear, and doable. If it sounds like fun to you, it's a great idea! Exercising 30–40 minutes at a moderate to high intensity pace (creating body sweat) can help release endorphins that create a feeling of euphoria. The more you move, the better your vibration moves. Should Yoga, Reiki, or Tai Chi be more up your alley, I stand and applaud you as well! These modalities center, strengthen, and balance your mind and body; they also raise your vibration and bring you into the moment. I personally find that meditating, immediately after Yoga, enhances my ability to have out of body experiences, and to astral travel also known as astral projection, and experience remote viewing.

11. Seek the Wisdom of Uplifting Mentors and Coaches

For many of us, it can be difficult to see the forest for the trees. We can be so focused on our current circumstances that we find ourselves unable to see alternatives. Mentors and coaches can provide that necessary perspective for us. Using their own experiences and wisdom, they can point us in the right direction to reach the success we desire in various areas of our lives. When it comes to tapping into our ability to release limiting beliefs of what is possible, and connect with the high frequency energy that surrounds and is part of us, a mentor can serve as a guide on our journey. Most of us would not go on a trip without some idea of where we are going. Mentors and coaches can provide that type of direction and assist us during the journey towards our destination.

12. Reverse the Flow

Can't sleep? Racing thoughts? Find a piece of the floor where you can lie on your back, with your bottom comfortably tucked up against the wall. Put your legs up the wall and reverse the blood flow in your body for 15 minutes. As your body relaxes, your mind will follow.

13. Use Natural Biodegradable Products for Body and Home

Our physical, emotional, and vibrational health is affected by everything that is put in, around, and on our body. The more we absorb chemical-based ingredients through our skin, such as makeup, soap, lotion, shampoo, conditioner, deodorant, sunscreen, perfume, and detergents, and inhale air freshener, disinfectant, bug spray, and cleaning products through our lungs, the harder our organs have to work to flush them out to achieve optimal health.

Therefore, the more natural the products are, the easier it is for our body to process, putting less of a strain on our organs. In some instances, such as regular use of coconut oil, it actually promotes a vibrant healthy body.

14. Replace Stinking Thinking

What happens when you continue to feel the emotional pain of your past, in the present moment, and see your life or the world through a harsh lens, believing love, empathy, compassion, togetherness, and unity cannot be achieved in your current life? Then that is what you will continue to find, perceive, experience, and reinforce while living your life at arm's length, limiting the magic of what is possible. Through the action of revisiting the tragic story of your past experience or experiences, over and over again, I propose that the person hurting you the most at this very moment is you!

This is what I refer to as *stinking thinking,* the debilitating power of holding onto the past. Giving the past meaning, as though it has meaning today, shows up in the experiences and choices you make today. With repeated visits to the pain of your past, you slug through the manure by holding on to it. Yes, it's familiar and can be used as justification for your current emotional pain, but it limits you from freely living your life to its full capability. The good news is that *stinking thinking* is an option. Release yourself from your hurtful thoughts of the past by following these suggested 15 steps. Leave the hurt where it belongs, in the past, and start living in the moment, with gratitude.

Do your thoughts or words start with, "I will be happy when" or, " I would be happy if?" Are your thoughts focused on the past or focused on a deficient future? Do you ever find yourself reliving a past conversation that included conflict, or inventing a harsh fictional conversation in your mind? If so, then you are not living in the present moment! This moment is all there truly is!

As you learn to observe yourself and notice your mind's thoughts engaging and going in the direction of *stinking thinking,* you are then able, through awareness and choice, to release them and bring yourself back into the present moment. By drawing your thoughts back into this very moment, you will transform your life into a far more liberating and joyous experience. Living in the moment can be as simple as noticing the inhale and exhale of your breath, or as calming as watching a bird glide in the upward and downward air currents as it glides freely and effortlessly with its environment. Living in the moment is living and being present to the beauty of your surroundings, as it opens the gates of a magical life, where the world is awaiting your command and to grant you your wishes!

As you monitor and become an observer of your own thoughts and the feelings associated with them, you begin to notice that the old story that previously played itself out through your words can now be eliminated from your vocabulary. You begin to feel lighter and calmer, as you are released from the shackles of the past that no longer have power over you. The power of your voice and the words you choose are now clear, precise, and specific as you mindfully speak with integrity—integrity that includes and goes beyond doing the right thing in a reliable way, but now includes the aspect of connection and oneness, knowing that you are the community, and the community is you.

15. Releasing Judgments and Giving Thanks

Is your life filled with peace, joy, and love? If the answer is yes, you need to know that just by being you, you raise the frequency vibration of other people around you!

You are an infinite perceiving being, who is in a body. As an infinite perceiving being, you have two things; you have the power of choice, and you have the power of awareness, an awareness that you receive from the universe, and your choice will always rule!

If you feel stuck in your environment there is one of two things going on. Either you have chosen your environment, or you have not addressed and cleared the judgments blocking you from changing it.

The universe receives your thoughts and words and responds accordingly, as though they are instructions of what you want brought into your life. Your judgments can keep you stuck! Which means you must question your judgments and be willing to be consciously aware enough to ask yourself: "Is what I just said true?"

Ask yourself, "If this judgment were not true, what are the possibilities of how it might affect my life?" Review how your judgments may be getting in your own way; question, release and replace them with higher vibrational thoughts of what you desire through the energy of thankfulness and gratitude for what you currently have and what you desire.

Many of these programmed judgments from your environment started when you were very young, and as you matured, you created and received judgments and conclusions of your very own from others by aligning, agreeing, resisting and reacting to them, and to the environment around you.

"You have to work hard to get ahead"

Why Increase Your Body Frequency and How?

"No pain, no gain"

"I could never approach that person, they are out of my league"

"I am to old to start over again"

"Rich people lie, cheat, or steal to get ahead"

"They shouldn't be doing that, they should act their age"

"Attractive people get all the breaks"

"I could never do that, I don't want to appear as selfish"

"I'm not successful until I own a home"

"I could never afford that"

"I have to work hard for my money"

"Why bother, the history of my past failures dictates my future"

These quotes are just a few examples of the judgments that have passed through my doors and hijacked my client's from reaching the higher frequencies that would help them manifest the life they desire. By releasing and replacing the old debilitating judgments with higher vibrational messages that include gratitude for what they already have, they were able to change their frequency and start to live the miraculous abundant life they desired.

What would you like to attract to your life? What would it look like? Once you have that vision clearly in your mind, remove the previous judgment from your thoughts and replace it with, "I am so thankful, grateful, and happy that I have this (then fill in the blank with your desire) in my life! By making this simple reprogramming adjustment, repeatedly, you will see the transition take place.

Activities That Lower Your Vibration and Disconnect You From Your Inner Spirit

Conversations that lack love and compassion; engaging in gossip, revenge, and vindictiveness; denying forgiveness; and rage.

Fear-based events, movies, and television shows, including the news and conversations.

Complaining, and blaming your life's problems on others or circumstances.

Taking a bath: Non-moving waterways, such as freshwater lakes, or taking a bath, actually deplete our body's energy vibration, and that is why we sleep so well after taking a bath.

Smoking/Alcohol/Prescription Drugs: alter your natural vibrational levels.

Consuming canned and processed foods: contain next to zero vibrational energy.

Drinking chlorinated, fluoridated water: treated or filtered city water generally contains fluoride. Fluoride is known to affect the functioning of the pineal gland. The pineal gland is the gateway to higher consciousness and a higher energy vibration.

Using chemical-based makeup, laundry detergent, soap, lotions, and cleaning products.

Continuous analytical thinking and activities that stifle your creativity.

Conclusion

If you believe you can do all things based on an infinite number of possibilities, you are correct! Mindful living and meditation are the vehicles that will enable you to enter into such an existence!

I live my life with complete confidence that once my clear and precise intention or thought is released from my mind, released into the living realm of possibilities, no matter how outrageous or impossible that thought or intention may seem, it happens. I experience the universe's response as it brings that thought or intention into physical form. This intelligent living dimension that I communicate with, and refer to as the Spirit World, can be explained through the science of quantum physics.

In the realm of quantum physics, it is in the act of observing something that literally influences the physical processes taking place, and the possibilities are infinite.

Deepak Chopra, in his "What is Consciousness?" video, explains quantum physics this way:

"The biggest mystery of our existence is our own existence.

Who are we?

Where do we come from?

Where do we go when we die?

Where is the soul; do we have one?

What is our true nature?

Living Supernatural in the Natural World

When we look closely, the true nature of our reality is revealed to us.

Looking closer than molecules and atoms, we enter the realm of quantum reality.

At this level of reality, there is no matter.

What we think of as tiny particles is actually not material at all but waves of potential.

The waves represent different potential outcomes of reality.

Only when observed does the wave collapse into one perceived outcome and is seen again as a particle.

The physical world as we see it is not reality; the true nature of reality is pure potential, infinite possibilities, and infinite creativity.

This true reality has no beginning and no end.

It does not exist in space and time; space and time exists within it.

This we call consciousness.

Our existence and the existence of everything we see is dependent on a conceptualizing consciousness.

This consciousness perceives, governs, constructs, and becomes the universe.

Our experience as beings within the universe is a continual activity within consciousness; what we experience as images, sensations, thoughts, emotions and feelings, are all qualities of consciousness.

Consciousness and its qualities are all that exists, and this is our true identity. We experience the world from our subjective point of view. We see objects and beings as existing in their own right, separate from us. This is an illusion.

In the end, we are all one consciousness that is simultaneous.

Conclusion

All observers, all modes of observation, and all objects of observation, I am that, you are that, all this is that, and that alone is.

We are not just a drop in the ocean; you are the mighty ocean in the drop."

How far away you are from source energy, the energy that created you, is how far you are out of synchronization with your life's purpose. The sooner you know your path, the sooner the universe will put everything into alignment for you to live the life you are designed to live.

The universe is always speaking to you. It is your job to pay attention to what is being said! It is important to realize there is no such thing as a coincidence. A coincidence is the universe giving you direction, telling you to pay attention. Another form of communication from the universe may be a gentle thought that runs through your mind, and might sound similar to: "Hmm, that's odd; that doesn't seem right," "That's interesting; that's the second time I heard that," or "Everywhere I go, that thing keeps showing up." This is the universe trying to get your attention. This is the universe responding to your thought or intention, giving you specific direction to take notice, and move the process along to bring your thought or intention into the physical world.

At first, the voice of the universe is quite gentle. However, if the message continues to fall on deaf ears, it tends to get louder and louder until it gives you an abrupt smack on the side of your head. If you still do not pay attention, it will try again with something that feels more like getting a brick up the side of your head. If that doesn't work, then the roof falls in on your head. In my case, it was a minivan, travelling seventy miles per hour, trying to fit through my tailpipe. That got my attention!

Life is about growth and change. When you are not in the process of growth and change, when you find yourself in a stagnant position without a vision of what to do, or where to go next, then relax, and bring your mind and body into the moment, and allow your thoughts to wander.

Daydream! Imagine what your perfect life, relationship, social state, or career would look like. Start with one area of your life that you would like to transition the most at this very moment. This thought of transition must be about you, not about another person's situation. The daydreaming visions of your life and the world in which you would like to live, are only limited by your imagination. Be as creative as you wish, releasing any of the *"yeah, but"* thoughts, as that will send mixed messages to the universe as to what you want.

When you think of an obstacle that could get in your way, or a challenge that would need to be overcome, the universe will respond by giving you that obstacle because that is the energy you released. Guide your daydream to exactly what you want, giving it as much detail as you can. Then listen, watch, and take notice of the gentle voice from the universe, guiding you as it transitions the world, by bringing your thoughts and intentions into reality.

The language of the universe also applies to the Third Law of Motion, which says for every action, there is an equal and opposite reaction. In other words, for every thought that you think, for every thought that you have that moves into action, it is going to create an equal and opposite reaction. The notion of *"do unto others as they will do unto you"* is incorrect! The Third Law of Motion dictates that the return of energy has already been put into motion with the original release of *intent*. Therefore, you have to take responsibility for the energetically transmitted thoughts and actions that you generate.

There is an energy field—an energy flow—that I strongly feel in my own life, and I know many other people feel as well. When I am in the flow of the universe, it feels like a gentle stream running through me with a sense of oneness, with all there ever was, is now, and the infinite possibilities of what can be. It feels open and free of restrictions or boundaries. I feel the presence of God within me!

I want to leave you with the following parable, which was written by an unknown author and has been making the rounds on the Internet, as well as having been published several times:

Life After Birth

In a mother's womb, there were two babies.

"Do you believe in life after delivery?" one twin asks the other.

Conclusion

"Why, of course. There has to be something after delivery. Maybe we are here to prepare ourselves for what we will be later," the other replies.

"Nonsense," says the first. *"There is no life after delivery. What kind of life would that be?"*

The second responds, *"I don't know, but it will be lighter than here. Maybe we will walk with our legs and eat with our mouths. Maybe we will have other senses that we can't understand now."*

The first replies, *"That is absurd. Walking is impossible. And eating with our mouths? Ridiculous! The umbilical cord supplies nutrition and everything we need. Life after delivery is to be logically excluded. The umbilical cord is too short."*

But the second insists, *"I think there is something, and maybe it's different than it is here. Maybe we won't need this physical cord anymore."*

The first replies, *"Nonsense. Moreover, if there is life, then why has no one ever come back from there? Delivery is the end of life. In the after-delivery, there is nothing but darkness and silence and oblivion. It takes us nowhere."*

"Well, I don't know," says the second, *"but certainly we will meet Mother, and she will take care of us."*

The first replies, *"Mother? You actually believe in Mother? That's laughable. If Mother exists, then where is she now?"*

The second says, *"She is all around us. We are surrounded by her. We are of her. It is in her that we live. Without her, this world would not and could not exist."*

"Ha," says the first, *"I do not see her, so it is only logical that she does not exist."*

But then the second twin answers, *"Sometimes, when I'm in silence and I focus, and I listen, I can perceive her presence, and I can hear her loving voice, calling down from above."*

Throughout this book, I have shared stories of my own life experiences in order to inspire you to explore your own abilities. Your ability to connect with the Spirit World, the physical world, and each other is only limited by your decision to stay within culturally accepted boundaries. You have the power to change your boundaries and extend them into the realm of endless possibilities.

It can be easy, like the first twin, to define your world simply by what your five senses tell you and ignore the possibility of anything beyond that. Yet, when you open your mind, like the second twin, you can step out in faith and a willingness to expand your mind beyond the experiences of your five senses. What I have called the Spirit World is something that lives inside us and is all around us. When you are open to the possibilities, your journey through this life can be even more magnificent than it is at this very moment.

Think of all the ways that you are already using your ability to connect with a larger world. There is your intuition: the little voice in your head that serves to caution you or provide butterflies in your stomach at the thought of a possibility to have an exciting experience or relationship. Your intuition is what provides the peace you feel when spending time in nature. These are all extensions of that ability, which can only grow with time, by paying attention to your thoughts, and the intention your thoughts create.

I want to point out, however, that while we all have this ability, using it is a matter of practice, to make it feel like a natural extension of yourself, a feeling that allows you to come to a deeper understanding of who you are and your place in this universe.

Throughout my life, I found that when I began to get angry or frustrated, the energy I released had a negative impact on the physical world around me, and the opposite was true when I released positive energy. You may have noticed that those who tend to give off positive energy are easier to be around. Individuals who give off negative energy tend to be more difficult to be around and can drain your energy.

Our world is dealing with multiple issues, and those issues are creating deep divisions among individuals, groups, and nations. The negative energy that grows between individuals deepens those divisions. When we make the conscious choice, however, to react with love instead of hate and anger, then

Conclusion

we can begin to understand each other on a whole other level. I know you have the power within you to make this shift of awareness!

For those of us who have lost loved ones, the grieving process can be difficult. By connecting with Spirit, you can understand that your loved ones are not *gone* but have transitioned from their physical form back into Spirit. Remember, we are all spiritual beings having a human experience!

I invite you to explore your own ability to connect with the Spirit World. Working with someone can help you to develop your skill set, so that you too can talk with the living Spirit World and learn to connect with other people through telepathy. You can also develop your ability to be empathetic so that you can learn to better sense the emotions of others.

Additionally, I have given you different exercises and activities to try on your own. There is, however, always more to discover and learn. The experiences I related in this book merely scratch the surface of what is possible. Opening yourself up to the possibilities is just the first of many steps that you can take on this journey.

I am excited to help you grow and expand your own human experience through a deeper connection with the Spirit World. Visit my website, www.dianewargalla.com, to learn more.

Wishing you the best on your path of discovery!

Diane Wargalla

Testimonials

"I have known Diane since we were young teenagers, and her visit in January 2016 was an enjoyable one, like many we have had in the past. During our friendship, Diane has always been very honest about her connection to the Spirit World.

However, the 2016 trip to Florida was different than anything else we have been through together. It was January 9th, 2016, when our phones sent us tornado warnings that sounded like air raid sirens.

We had been at our clubhouse, in our mobile home park, attending a dinner event; upon arriving back in our home, we turned on the television for news on the storm, and it was then that we turned on the Weather Channel. It was unnerving to see three dots, representing tornadoes, being shown in the Fort Myers area where we were physically, and we were right in the middle of the storm. This is our home away from home, for almost six months of the year. Diane sat on the couch in front of the television with her legs tucked underneath her, which could only be described as looking like a Buddha. It seemed as if she wasn't upset or stressed out at all, but simply watching the dots with a relaxed body. I watched the Weather Channel and started seeing the dots disappear. The storm that had seemed so intense just a short time ago was now losing strength. I changed the channel, and we all started getting back to other topics of conversation, and relaxing.

Twenty minutes later, the sirens went off again, and Diane asked for the television to be turned back to the Weather Channel. I didn't understand why she was just not content to join us in our conversation. When I said I wasn't going to do it, I was surprised at how intense her request was to see the Weather Channel again.

I hadn't realized that she was connecting with the storm but really thought that I was helping her to not dwell on something that we couldn't control. However, she didn't give up, and I finally turned on the Weather Channel with its satellite image of the storm as one large dot directly above us.

Diane slipped back into a relaxed, meditative state, sitting herself on the sofa. It was mesmerizing as I watched the storm on the television. Even as it was pounding on my home, we watched as it moved out of our immediate location to a less populated area. The storm passed, and we found out that there was little property damage, but most importantly, no life was lost.

Afterwards, Diane and I had a deep conversation, and she explained her intentions, which helped me to understand what she was doing.

Fast forward to September 11th, 2017, when Hurricane Irma was expected to bear down as a category five storm, with a direct hit on Fort Myers, Florida, with the water levels expected to rise eight to ten feet. I remembered this experience and couldn't help but ask Diane if there was anything she could do to divert it. It was really a long-shot because I didn't know if she could help. After all, the last time, she had been in the thick of the storm, but now, she was almost 2,000 miles away.

Although I had been thinking of calling her, I did not. Shortly thereafter, as a result of her catching the details on the radio, it was she who called me to see if everything was alright.

As we spoke, Diane indicated she was in the process of accessing Hurricane Irma details on her computer. She burst out laughing, making reference to its enormous size, just as I was asking her if there was anything she could do with it. At first, I thought she was laughing at my request, but then she explained that she was laughing because she was excited at the opportunity to mimic the story of Moses from the Bible, declaring she was going to go biblical! My understanding was that her intent was to be a part of the energy force that would redirect the waters, with minimal damage to properties, and move the direction of Hurricane Irma away from Fort Myers.

Testimonials

Diane asked how I felt my home would make out in the storm, and I told her I felt my home would be fine. She told me to hold onto that feeling, and that's what I did.

There were reports and photos of Hurricane Irma receding the water away from the shoreline as far as the eye could see, returning back to the normal heights, with minimal surges in the two to three-foot range, which was considered unusually low. Another aspect of Hurricane Irma that was unusual was its sudden change in direction, along with a decrease of wind speeds. According to computer generated projections, meteorologist reports indicated this was something that was unexplainable and unheard of.

While it is one thing to hear about someone having the ability to influence weather, it is something different to see the results yourself—not once but twice.

From these experiences, I believe that there is more than what we can see with our five senses.

No one can ever know how much I appreciate Diane's efforts, but more importantly, I appreciate the fact that she is showing us there is a way to connect with our world on a deeper level."

Darlene Patrick
Bobcaygeon, Ontario

"I was sitting on the couch, flipping through an unread newspaper, and Diane was sitting in a chair across from me, chatting with a friend who was sitting beside me. Suddenly diverting from her conversation with our friend, Diane looked at me and asked if the picture I was looking at in the paper was the Leaning Tower of Pisa.

The newspaper was folded over with a picture of a building leaning over on a forty-five-degree angle. This was a picture of a hotel damaged during an earthquake in Taiwan the previous day.

Living Supernatural in the Natural World

What startled me most about her inquiry, was not that I was looking at the picture of the hotel that was leaning over just like the Tower of Pisa, but that the picture was facing me while another page of the newspaper was facing Diane, who was sitting across from me, several feet away, and the picture of the hotel was blocked from her view. Realizing that the newspaper in my hand was several layers thick, it struck me that she was seeing the picture through another means other than through sight.

Astonished, I showed our guest the photo she was talking about, just to confirm to him that she had no way of seeing the photograph. We were both amazed by her ability to perfectly describe the photograph I was holding in my hand. As we both laughed, trying to get our heads around the fact she was able to see the picture that was completely blocked from her normal sight, she said: "What?" I explained it to her, and then she laughed.

This is just one of the many examples of her special gifts and connection to the Spirit World. Even after many years, Diane continues to surprise and astonish me.

She has such a strong personal energy field that she can affect and impact the mechanical, electrical, as well as nearby electronics. For example, one time we were on the phone while she was sitting in her car, and we had an argument. Diane got so fired up and agitated while she was sitting in the parking lot of a mall that her car would not start. I joined her in the parking lot, and we waited for a tow truck to arrive during a late-night snow storm. The mechanic later confirmed that the relatively new car battery had been fried and needed to be replaced!

In another instance, we were in a cellular store where Diane was looking for help with her cell phone. They kept telling her there didn't seem to be anything wrong with the phone. They started getting impatient with her, and I thought to myself, "Oh, Oh! Watch out!" Then it happened. The entire store went dark and all the lighting and computer systems crashed. "That'll teach them!" I thought to myself. They eventually fixed her cell phone.

Which reminds me of our first date: It was a warm summer's night in Port Credit. We went for a walk along the boardwalk so that Lucy, her dog, could stretch her legs after patiently waiting in the car during our dinner date. As we

Testimonials

walked by the marina, I noticed the street light just ahead go out. As we approached it, the next street light also went out. By the time we approached the third street light along the boardwalk, which also went out, I turned towards Diane, and I looked into her eyes and asked her, "Is there something you want to tell me?" She admitted she was nervous. I told her there was nothing to be nervous about. We continued our walk and no more lights went out! I figured that our date cost the city a couple of thousand dollars that night. She can also willingly exercise control on electrical objects. One night, she came to my apartment and announced excitedly that she had been able to turn the street lamps on and off in the parking lot of my building, with her thoughts. We went down to the parking lot, and I pointed to different lights, and she proceeded to shut them off and power them up at will.

She is often heard speaking to inanimate objects, such as power tools and riding lawn mowers, and getting them to start after I have given up in frustration. She is soothing and comes from a place of love and support as she talks the machinery into cooperating!

It was from this place of love and soothing that she spoke to the tsunami that was approaching us during our vacation in Hawaii, in 2011. As she later told me, she was talking to the massive wave and sending it love, positive energy, and calming reassurance as it approached the island. All I could see in the moment was Diane standing on a small balcony, eyes slightly open, hands gently moving in a circular motion as she was in a deep meditative state.

In the background, I could hear a CNN reporter on location at the dormant Diamond Head volcano, which was visible a couple of miles away to my left from where we were standing on the fourteenth-floor hotel balcony, telling listeners to get ready for the big wave that was expected to hit shore at any time. Twice, I saw the water recede from the marina directly below us, and the yachts were left sitting on the bare sand as the ocean was literally sucked away from the shore for a couple of hundred yards, as seen by the trail of illuminating lights outlining the hotel property and marina directly in front of us. I braced for the tsunami to come ashore any moment, as did the reporter, who was excitedly jabbering away on the TV in the background.

It never happened! The water quietly lapped at the shore and slowly came back in; the yachts rose back to their normal level, bobbing gently on the water.

The reporter was saying this was incredible, and asked the local meteorologist, who only moments earlier had provided updates of the tsunami's location being directly offshore, for an explanation. Of course, he didn't have one.

They just filled the air with a bunch of nonsensical babble. Once the water receded for the second time before returning to normal levels, Diane came out of her meditative state and explained how she had connected in with and worked with thousands of local Hawaiian energy workers and healers, along with tens of thousands of other energy workers from around the world, to literally calm the waters.

It was later reported the tsunami had bounced through the channels of the Hawaiian Islands, on its path to the U.S. West Coast, with minimal damage. There was no loss of life or property damage, except for one home that was washed out to sea.

On another occasion, I witnessed Diane's commitment to protect Fort Myers and the state of Florida from Hurricane Irma's destructive force. In the days leading up to its arrival to the U.S., I watched Diane sit in a meditative state and connect with the hurricane's energy. Her plan was to have the waters recede from Florida's shores and change the hurricane's trajectory inland to minimize the water damage, especially to her friend's mobile home in Fort Myers.

To another person, this might appear to be impossible; however, on the evening following Hurricane Irma's crossing the Florida Keys and making landfall in the state of Florida, I watched as the meteorologist from CNN reported that Hurricane Irma veered away from the expected path outlined on a simulated computer trajectory, from only twenty-four hours earlier.

The CNN reporter explained how the hurricane altered its course and followed a path that was far less damaging to the Western coast of Florida than was expected, with virtually no sea surge damage, which had been expected to be in the order of nine feet or so, and he gave full credit to human intervention through prayer. He said there was no other earthly explanation for why Irma had deviated from the projected path.

Testimonials

He closed by noting the U.S. meteorological service in Atlanta was checking their computer systems to figure out why they were so inaccurate with their weather modeling predictions! Our friend's mobile home escaped virtually unscathed.

I have witnessed her interventions with nature, including calming and relocating tornadoes in Florida, and creating a violent wind storm that came up from underneath our feet at the Peace Valley Sanctuary, which was followed by the immediate arrival of the U.S. Air Force to investigate the phenomena.

Our time together has been an extension of our first date, comprised of a variety of supernatural adventures involving an invisible living world that Diane is completely in tune with.

Diane constantly amazes me and others as she comes from a place of love and forgiveness. Whether in the same room or miles away, she has a big heart, and her empathetic nature picks up on other people's pain and suffering through their anger, tears, and fears, and she openly and compassionately gives empathy, inspiration, and support. She is an amazing human being, living her life connected to the world in a way the average person is not, but can be!"

Jack Di Nardo
Toronto, Ontario

"I recently had the opportunity to connect with a great uncle of mine who was a ship's captain on a Great Lakes freighter, which was sunk in 1913 during what was called, 'The Great Storm.'

I was aware of Diane Wargalla's claim of being able to serve as a medium and connect with people who have passed away.

As there were a number of questions associated with the disaster of the 1913 storm, I thought that if Diane actually had the abilities that she claimed to have, then this might be the perfect time to put them to the test.

Living Supernatural in the Natural World

I have known Diane for many years and have enjoyed her company as a friend. But candidly, I never really bought into her claims to be able to communicate with those who have passed away. She refers to it as the Spirit World.

However, given that I had nothing to lose, I suggested that we try out this gift and clear up some of the mysteries associated with my great-uncle's ship sinking.

We went to the Huron County Museum in Goderich, where they had an exhibition dedicated to the Great Storm.

Among other artifacts on display, they had my uncle's pocket watch and his personal diary.

Diane immediately went to them and focused deeply on these items for a few minutes. Shortly thereafter, she asked me to come and take notes, as she relayed messages from my Great-Uncle Ed.

She began to say things that pertained to the moments of the storm. They were not general, vague things but rather detailed comments that shed a brand-new light on the event.

One such event was the presence of a pirate ship there that day, and that they ordered Ed's ship to drop anchor. No one has ever been able to answer why Ed would have dropped his anchor under such conditions.

Ed told Diane that his rudder had broken off, and that caused him to lose control of the ship. Diane said she didn't know what a rudder was but simply reported that it was what Ed had told her.

During the connection session, Diane experienced a severe pain in her right wrist, about three to four inches above the wrist on the right arm. That is the exact location where I broke my arm as an 11-year-old.

There were a number of items raised during the connection that can be verified by other sources, and I will be following those up in the months ahead.

Testimonials

Too much information was shared that was true, which Diane could not have known ahead of this session.

After the session ended, the museum offered to let us see a video that aired on the Discovery Channel about the Great Storm. We sat down to watch it, and we both gasped when the video revealed that my uncle's ship had been found on the floor of Lake Huron, lying on its side. The rudder had been broken off!

This was an absolutely amazing experience for me, and the doubts that I had prior to the experience have gone away.

I believe, without a shadow of a doubt, Diane has, without question, the ability to connect with the Spirit World."

Robert (Bob) McConkey
Brantford, Ontario, Canada, January 21, 2016.

About the Author

Diane Wargalla is an author, medium, empath, mentor, and entrepreneur.

Taking the principles from the latest scientific research in quantum physics, Diane translates this seemingly obscure branch of science and puts it into profoundly exciting practical application for daily living, so it becomes as natural as breathing. This is how she lives her life, and believes once her translation is understood, it not only can, but it will be, the catalyst that transforms your entire life and allows you to live the life you desire, should you "choose" to.

Diane's ability to make a difference in other people's lives and manifest her life, including her previous career where she led the National Communications Group for Citigroup, the largest financial institution in the world at the time, has led to many remarkable breakthroughs and achievements. This included her promotion to management at Citicorp, where she led a national team across Canada.

Born in Toronto, Ontario, Diane feels most at home on the Southern shores of Nova Scotia visiting her relatives and is a descendant of First Nations Métis. Diane has an innate knowing that she has a deep connection and unity with all that surrounds her in the universe, as a natural way of being. What she has also discovered is, that this is a foundational concept of First Nations philosophy.

Diane was personally invited by world renowned scientist Dr. William Tiller, who appeared in "What the Bleep Do We Know!?", to be a member of the Psychotronics Society of America and participate in his Consciousness Field Project. The Consciousness Field Project was developed by Deepak Chopra and the Merraki Institute. This 18-month research project utilized research from Dr. Tiller and Dr. Gabriele Hilberg, merging the fields of psychology, physics, and consciousness.

Diane is well versed and experienced in assisting you to create the breakthroughs you desire and develop your abilities to access information that comes through from other dimensions of reality.

She works with individuals to help them to recognize their own natural abilities, the ones that work in concert with and beyond their own five senses. Her knowledge and skill can help you to explore the next part of your amazing life's journey!

Diane is an accomplished public speaker who uses her powerful storytelling skills to reach out and touch the child-like curiosity that lies with each of us. She speaks to your innate wisdom as you polish and develop your skills, as well as exploring your natural abilities.

Diane currently lives in Canada. Through her work with individuals, video series, and writing, Diane invites you to join her in connecting with the physical and Spirit World that surrounds and connects us as one!